GOOD NEWS FROM AFRICA

Series Preface

Regnum Resources for Mission provides helpful material to mission practitioners, in both foundational and practical topics.

The paper used for the text of this book Forest Stewardship Council (FSC) Certified

GOOD NEWS FROM AFRICA
COMMUNITY TRANSFORMATION THROUGH THE CHURCH

Edited by Brian Woolnough

Regnum Resources
for Mission

Copyright © OCMS 2013

First published 2013 by Regnum Books International

Regnum is an imprint of the Oxford Centre for Mission Studies
St. Philip and St. James Church, Woodstock Road, Oxford, OX2 6HR, UK
www.ocms.ac.uk/regnum

09 08 07 06 05 04 03 8 7 6 5 4 3 2 1

The right of Brian Woolnough to be identified as the editor of this work
has been asserted by him in accordance with the Copyright, Designs
and Patents Act 1988.

All rights reserved. No part of this publication may be reproduced, stored in a retrieval system, or transmitted, in any form or by any means, electronic, mechanical, photocopying, recording or otherwise, without the prior permission of the publisher or a license permitting restricted copying. In the UK such licenses are issued by the Copyright Licensing Agency, 90 Tottenham Court Road, London W1P 9HE.

British Library Cataloguing in Publication Data
A catalogue record for this book is available from the British Library

ISBN: 978-1-908355-33-1

Typeset in Palatino by WORDS BY DESIGN
Cover design by WORDS BY DESIGN
Printed and bound in Great Britain
for Regnum Books International by 4edge Ltd, Hockley, Essex.

Dedication

To all those working to bring God's love to those living in poverty around the world. Especially to those who have befriended and inspired me whilst working with Tearfund and OCMS.

Contents

    Preface   ix

1. The Growth of the 'Development Business' and Christian Transformation   1
   Brian Woolnough, OCMS
2. Sustainable Development, Through Mobilising Churches   11
   Donald Mavunduse, Tearfund
3. Listening to the Poor, in Microfinance   25
   Irene Mutalima, Zambia
4. Engaging with the Community, the Fight against AIDS   41
   Joshua Banda, Zambia
5. Networking Local Churches, for HIV/AIDS Interventions   55
   Francis Mkandawire, Malawi
6. Satisfying the Thirsty, by Water and Sanitation Projects   69
   Kenneth Twinamatsiko, Uganda
7. Transforming Communities, Through Education   81
   Philippe Ouedraogo, Burkina Faso
8. A Bottom-Up Perspective, for Transforming Communities   91
   Fanen Ade, Nigeria
9. Caring for Our Sisters, Comforting the Abused   103
   Jennifer Singh, Uganda and Ethiopia
10. Conclusions and Outstanding Questions   115
    Brian Woolnough, OCMS

    Select Bibliography   125

PREFACE

This is a book which I have wanted to produce for well over a decade!

In 1999 I spent a month working in Zambia on a Tearfund Transform team. We were working with the Zambian Prison Fellowship, helping to build a clinic for Lusaka Central Prison. That month changed my life, as I met African Christians there whose life and faith put mine to shame, and met and started to understand the lives of many Zambian locals.

I thought that I understood the world quite well. I had been working professionally at the University of Oxford and had had the privilege of travelling to many countries around the world for conferences on science education, speaking, researching and discussing the finer points of physics education. I had been to over 40 countries, most in highly beautiful and exotic places, but in hindsight I realised that I had been to just *one* country – a middle-class, western country, which just happened to be meeting in different venues. In Zambia I met a different group of people, who were typical of about 80% of the world. They were relatively poor but they were warm, resilient, and compassionate and largely had a simple but practical faith in their living God. They lived their lives totally, holistically, as to the Lord.

Subsequently, I had the privilege of working with Tearfund's International Team, and had the opportunity of meeting many of their partners in Asia and in Africa, sharing in their work with the local communities serving and caring for them in their need. In each case I found local Indians, Nepalese, Philippines, Thais, and Africans leading their local CNGOs (Christian Non-Governmental Organisations). They were highly professional, totally committed to serving the poor and their Lord, and doing development work of the highest quality. I kept encouraging them to write up their work so that others might learn from their experience, but they rarely did. They were practitioners, too busy working on their next project to spend time writing up their last one!

After six years with Tearfund I went to work at OCMS where I met many more church leaders from around the world, many of them involved with development work in their own countries. Many were already familiar with the work of Tearfund. However, these folk were too busy with their work back home, and now their new research degree work, to have time to write up what they were doing.

Eventually I have been able to persuade eight of my friends, through Tearfund and OCMS, to write up some of their work so that we can proclaim a composite message – the good news that development work is fit and well in many parts of the world, in particular as it is done with and through the local church – God's chosen means of transforming the world. It fits in appropriately to Regnum's Resources for Mission Series.

It is my joy to celebrate and disseminate such work with the hope that others may find their examples, and some underlying issues discussed, helpful. This book is dedicated to the lives and work of the contributors, and many others like them, serving God and the poor through their church.

BEW
April 2013

THE GROWTH OF THE 'DEVELOPMENT BUSINESS' AND CHRISTIAN TRANSFORMATION

BRIAN WOOLNOUGH

Brian Woolnough is Research Tutor, OCMS, previously with Tearfund and the University of Oxford's Department of Educational Studies.

THE GROWTH OF THE DEVELOPMENT MOVEMENT

One of the most remarkable developments over the last half century has been the growth of the aid and development business, in which people from the materially rich countries (MRC) in the western world provide money and resources to those living in poverty and distress in the poorer countries. The rich have sought to help the poor. Vast amounts of money have been transferred from the more developed countries to the less developed ones. Multinational organisations have been set up such as the UN, the World Bank, the IMF, and the WHO. Most countries have an international aid programme, e.g. USAID, DFID. Many non-governmental organisations (NGOs) have been set up to tackle specific problems. Most church denominations and faith groups have similar programmes. Many rich individuals commit their money and energies to helping the poor. Issues of health, poverty, education, children at risk, sexual and physical oppression, injustice, and natural and man-made disaster have been tackled. Some of these programmes have been enormously beneficial. Inevitably, much of this money has been wasted.

One of the most encouraging developments within the Christian church has been the growth of the concept of holistic, or integral, mission where God's command to his church has been to tackle all aspects of life – the material, the emotional, and the environmental – as well as the spiritual. This has always been a strong aspect of the church's work, from the teaching of the Old Testament into the early church, through to the Catholic traditions, the Salvation Army, and the evangelical reformers (to give just some examples). In the first half of the twentieth century the evangelical church had shied away from the 'social gospel' and concentrated on the primacy of 'saving souls' to the exclusion of caring for the poor and needy. Indeed it took considerable debate in the Lausanne conference of 1974 before John Stott and Christian leaders from the developing world could persuade the evangelical church about the God-given commission that all Christians had the responsibility to care for bodies as well as souls, and that the holistic gospel must be directed to the whole person as well as the state of the whole community.

THE PROBLEMS, THE HINDRANCES TO DEVELOPMENT

And yet there still remains a vast number of people living in poverty (over one billion people, about one sixth of the world, live on less than $1 per day); gross inequality still exists between the rich and the poor (in many ways this inequality has got worse in financial terms), and vast numbers of folk still live in material and spiritual poverty. In Africa in particular, the problem of extreme poverty has seemed intransient.

It has been suggested that the problems of underdevelopment are too large, too expensive, to be solved. But compared to other expenditures of rich governments they are trivial. It has been agreed internationally that if all countries spent less than 1% of their GNP on aid (in fact 0.7%) the problems of ending chronic poverty could be solved... *for ever*. At a time when the US and UK spend $710 billion and $55 billion respectively on military expenditure, compared to $23 billion and $12 billion on non-military aid, it is hard to ague that countries are not rich enough to solve the problem of world poverty.

This is not the place to discuss the underlying reasons for the perseverance of such inequalities, but they might be considered under the following headings:
- Bad governance, corruption and mis-management in receptor countries;
- Unjust financial systems imposed by rich, donor countries;
- Lack of political will by governments and people;
- Civil wars within countries;
- Money given with inappropriate conditions attached due to vested interests;
- Inhospitable physical and climatic conditions, especially with climate changes;
- Indifference, selfishness and sin throughout the world.

Recently, some commentators have been suggesting that not only has this aid been inefficiently used but that it has been positively detrimental - it has done more harm than good. Books referring to 'Dead Aid' describe how aid can cause dependency and bad governance, and actively prevent indigenous development. More disturbing still, certain Christian commentators suggest that Christians, although acting out of the best possible motives, can produce a situation 'When Helping Hurts'.

WHAT DO WE MEAN BY DEVELOPMENT?

The Commission for Africa report had a telling paragraph answering the 'big question'.

> *(Ask) what is development for? (And) you get very different answers in different cultures. Many in western countries see it as being about places like Africa 'catching up' with the developed world. In Africa, by contrast, you are more likely to be told something to do with well-being, happiness and membership of community.*

Many in the west see development largely in secular terms, helping individuals become richer, less materially poor. But Christian development work has aims far deeper than that and seeks to relieve folk from both material and spiritual poverty; it seeks to transform communities, and help its members become more whole people, developed in body, mind and spirit. It is interesting to compare the two:

Type of donor aid	Secular	Christian
Goals	Material wellbeing.	Holistic wellbeing
Focus	Individual	Community
World view	Maintenance of western, consumerist values	'Justice for the poor' Prv 29:7
Objectives	Set by donor	'Listening to the poor'
Relationships	Donor dominated, top-down	Genuine partnership, bottom-up
Underlying philosophy	Support vested interests of western donor	Focus only on what benefits local people

E.g. Micro credit schemes	Making profit on 'banking model' for entrepreneurial poor	Helping the 'poorest of the poor'
Decision making	Made by donors	Made by local communities

ROLE OF THE LOCAL CHURCH?

There are two alternative attitudes towards the role of the local churches in relation to development work among the poor – *either* leave the development work to the professional experts who have the skills and expertise required (whereas the local church does not) *or* work in and through the local church which is God's chosen instrument for meeting the needs of the local community. The early church certainly took the latter approach. This is the stance that Tearfund, and an increasing number of other CNGOs are taking. Indeed Tearfund has a slogan:

> *We are Christians passionate about the local church bringing justice and transforming lives – overcoming global poverty.*

In this book we will be illustrating through practical examples where God is, and has in the past been, using the church in different aspects of development to transform the lives of many. This really is good news from Africa. The local church really can be 'the hope of the world'.

WHY IS THE CHURCH SO PIVOTAL?
- Primarily, because 'it is there', a social structure throughout most of the needy countries of the world in daily contact with the poor.
- Indeed, churches are themselves part of the poor, and thus readily empathise with them.
- The church will remain there, long after relief organisations have gone home, and thus resolves the problem of sustainability.
- It has as its core mission to care for the poor and needy.
- It's ministers and pastors carry authority with the people in a way that distant political leaders never can.
- The church can provide volunteers.
- The church can immediately recognise the local needs and respond to them.

- The church system can provide a fantastic 'amplification factor'.

The church is able to provide an 'amplification factor' because of its very structure. This struck me very graphically when visiting Malawi recently to see how a Tearfund grant related to HIV/AIDS work was being implemented. I met the Tearfund partner, EAM (Evangelical Alliance of Malawi), who took me out to one of the villages to meet with eleven of the local pastors and about 200 members of their congregations. They told me of their work on HIV/AIDS education and care, and the associated general health education, and demonstrated through dance and drama ways that they were getting their messages across to their neighbours. The vigour and humour involved in their drama was transparent in any language. They also allowed me to join them on some of their sick visiting.

The Tearfund grant went to EAM who appointed one co-ordinator for each of the 21 regions in Malawi. I visited the Ntchisi region, where Mathias was the co-ordinator. Through him the church was able to contact about 10,000 Malawians – some 'amplification factor'!

- One EAM regional co-ordinator (Mathias), working with
- 11 pastors, who represented
- 40 churches, which covered
- 148 villages, where they were able to produce from their congregations about
- 400-plus trained volunteers, who were able to work with about 25 folk each, i.e.
- 10,000 Malawians.

It has been said that many philanthropists, such as the most generous and well-motivated Bill Gates, and many national and international aid organisations, would give their right arms to have an infrastructure like the church permeating the needy world through which they could work.

There are, of course, certain reasons why, in certain situations, the local church is not effective at meeting the needs of the poor and needy in the community:

- the local church is not geographically close to the need – though it is unlikely that there will be no needy folk in their proximity;
- the local church does not have the biblical vision to care for their poor and needy;

- the needs are too great for the local church – and in the case of traumatic disasters this may be so and expertise and resources of outsiders will be needed;
- the particular needs may be outside the expertise of the local church – certain technical, health and abuse problems may also benefit from additional help, but again the church should be ready to accept and welcome in the outsider, the refugee, and the abused;
- the local church may not be able to solve all the problems – but being alongside and sharing suffering with the needy is an important part of the work of God's church;
- the church is too busy 'preaching the gospel' and seeking conversion – but Jesus taught and demonstrated a holistic gospel, and the love of God embraces physical as well as spiritual needs.

HOW DO WE KNOW WE ARE MAKING A DIFFERENCE?

Accountability is one of the central principles of modern society. Whether we are talking about education, healthcare, government, or public welfare, the accountant's mind insists that we should be accountable to them. The development world has not escaped this trend and, not unreasonably, is required to look seriously at, and justify to others, how well their money and resources have been spent. The problems arise as to how best to evaluate the value of such development projects and to study the effect of such interventions. Should we evaluate using quantitative or qualitative methods? Modern practice is to emphasise the former, but whilst seeking to measure the impact of development projects by quantitative methods sounds attractive, it can lead to many problems:

- Can you measure what you are trying to change?
- Can you ensure that you do not over-emphasise what you can measure and forget other changes which cannot be measured?
- Can broad development objectives such as spiritual transformation be measured?
- Does reliability of measurement take undue precedence over validity?
- Can you be sure that any changes that have occurred can be attributed to the development project? Does correlation equate with causation?

- Who are we accountable to – the donor or the poor?
- Who is doing the evaluation – the donor or the recipient?

Whilst evaluation of any development work can be beneficial, this can usually be done much better by qualitative reflection of those involved (seeking to improve their own practice), rather than by trying to provide proof for external donors (by measuring the easily measurable factors). The inclusion of case studies, such as personal stories of transformation, can be much more informative and valid than hard quantitative measurements.

BIBLICAL JUSTIFICATION FOR INVOLVEMENT WITH RELIEF AND DEVELOPMENT

It may seem strange to many readers that a book on Christian development work needs a section outlining the biblical justification for getting involved with the local poor and needy. Is it not obvious and self-evident? Is it not natural for Christians to share God's love with those around them, especially those in need? But it must be recognised that some Christians, and some churches, in giving attention to spiritual needs, by concentrating almost exclusively on evangelism and the saving and developing of souls, have neglected the social and material needs of their neighbours. So let us consider what the Bible teaches about God's attitude to the poor, and what his expectations are for his people in this regard.

The outstanding message throughout the Bible is that God has great compassion for the needs of the poor, and hates injustice.

From the beginning, in the story of the children of Israel, we find God fighting their cause through Moses and Joshua, demanding that the oppressors 'Let my people go'. In Deuteronomy we find God establishing laws to ensure that 'there should be no poor among you' (Deut 15:4). Throughout the prophets we hear continued condemnation of those who oppress the poor (despite often claiming that they worship God – Isaiah 58) and prophecies that the Messiah will come 'to bring good news to the poor, bind up the broken-hearted, and proclaim freedom for the captive' (Isaiah 61:1-3).

When Jesus came, to be born among the poor, he took on this role of bringing good news to the poor for himself (Luke 4:14-19), and his most forthright parables teach the vital need for his followers to care for their poorer neighbours – see the parables of the Good Samaritan (Luke 10:25-

37), the Sheep and the Goats (Matt 25:31-46), and the Rich Man and Lazarus (Luke 16:19-31). Indeed it is these three parables where Jesus declares severest judgement on those who ignore the needs of the poor.

When we look at the example of the early church in the New Testament we see that they had 'all things in common' to support the poor (Acts 2:44-45), and that the Church of Macedonia even collected money for fellow Christians who were suffering from famine in far away countries (2 Cor 8:1-4). The letters of the writers to the early church consistently urge them to care for the poor, the widows and the fatherless (e.g. Galations 6:1, James 2:14-17, 1 John 3:7).

To conclude from the Bible that God is indifferent to the needs of the poor, indeed might even see poverty as an indication of God's displeasure with them, is a grossly distorted piece of exegesis.

OUTSTANDING QUESTIONS

The main theme throughout this book is that development work can usually best be done through the local church, God's people living and working in their community, fulfilling his command and following his example. Many individual Christians, many Christian NGOs, and many churches are doing just that. We will see and celebrate examples of this 'being Jesus in these places'. In so doing we will continue to ask questions about what is working well and what needs to be improved – fundamental questions such as:

- What do we mean by development?
- How does our world view, our theology, affect our aims and actions?
- What are the strengths and limitations of church-based development?
- How can the different 'actors' in development best relate?
- How can we best evaluate our work?
- How can well-meaning 'outsiders' best help?

The following contributions, written by Christian practitioners who are giving their lives to serve the poor in Africa, will give insights into many of these questions, and demonstrate ways that God's love is being brought to the poor and needy in a highly effective way. They cover a range of sub-Sahara African countries and a range of development activities: education, water and sanitation, microfinance, HIV/AIDS, community development and abused women. An Umoja approach is highlighted.

They are all working in and are from the African continent and are the most appropriate people to share, first-hand, this good news from Africa. I am the only westerner in the team but have had the privilege over the last decade or so to have shared their work with them personally. I have been inspired by their quality of Christian living and Christ-like service. Christians in the west have a lot to learn from the African world. It has been my joy and inspiration to share some of their stories in this book.

SUSTAINABLE DEVELOPMENT, THROUGH MOBILISING CHURCHES
DONALD MAVUNDUSE

Donald Mavunduse is the Head of East and Southern Africa, Tearfund.

From 1996 to 1999 I was employed as a manager in one of the largest Christian relief and development agency in the world. I looked after an integrated development programme in Mt. Darwin - a remote, largely dusty northern district of Zimbabwe. The budget was US$ 2 million per year. We worked with poor communities, with traditional chiefs and their helpers called *Sabhuku*. We also worked with local ward counsellors. We did not work with local churches.

One hot November afternoon, two church leaders from local Anglican and Church of Christ congregations arrived in my office without appointments. They wanted to understand why the organisation I worked for had stopped working with churches. I told them we were concerned about the church's low capacity and also potential problems with impartiality.

Two years later I remembered this conversation whilst driving a critically ill relative and looking for help. My relative had spent days unattended on a wooden bench in a government hospital in Harare. The 1,200 bed medical facility, perched on a small hill, had little medicine and patients had to bring their own drips. Some slept under beds or in corridors, and nurses were overwhelmed and snappy. We discharged our relative, but the only place we knew he could receive good medical attention was a mission hospital, 200km away. After a three-hour drive I parked my pick-up at its main reception, and immediately two male nurses rushed to attend to us.

As a family in our time of need we turned to the institution with over 100 years experience providing high level health and education services in Africa – the same institution we had had serious doubts as to whether could deliver grassroots development!

It took working for my current employer Tearfund UK 14 years later to appreciate that the church, including the local congregations, had the potential to provide credible community development.

THE TEARFUND APPROACH

Tearfund is a UK-based Christian relief and development organisation. While there has always been a strong focus and a lot of support to the work of the church, it was not until 2007 that a vision statement was explicit about Tearfund's work through local churches. Tearfund's vision is:

> *To see 50 million people released from material and spiritual poverty though a world wide network of 100,000 local churches.*

Before the new vision was agreed, there were encouraging developments from communities in Kenya, Uganda and Tanzania. Local churches and communities had been organised to respond to the needs of poverty and deprivation. Using a specific method called Church and Community Mobilisation Process (CCMP), also known as Umoja, poor people pooled their own resources to construct clinics and schools. Many of them lived on less than one dollar per day. The first community to go through this proactive process was a Maasai community in Narok, Kenya. The Maasai, who traditionally shunned modern education, were as a result of this process willing to sell part of their livestock to built schools for their children.

Elevating and mobilising the local church through Umoja helped to affirm Tearfund's Christian identity. It also had practical development significance, and addressed the perennial, elusive questions:

> *Is the change sought for the poor meaningful? And will it last?*

For change to be meaningful, Tearfund's vision argues it has to be holistic – it has to be more than improving economic or physical well-being for the poor. It has to improve relationships, dignity and spiritual well-being. In other words, it's both about what the poor communities achieve (such as better health or education) and who they become (more tolerant of other views, confident to solve own problems, compassionate about the poor).

For change to last it has to be supported by sustainable institutions that enable communities to achieve more or to help them should they fall on hard times. Tearfund recognised that apart from government structures in Africa, the church is the only other institution with a permanent presence that does not depend on external funding. Local congregations, including those whose buildings are of mud walls and remote, are part of an extensive network of churches connected at village, national, regional and international level.

These are unique strengths that the church brings to community development. Strengths that enable Umoja (the strategy where the local churches are mobilised and encouraged to work with, and for, their local communities) to help deliver on the questions of impact and sustainability.

UMOJA IN ACTION

The African Inland Church of Tanzania (AICT) has implemented Umoja since 1998 across 15 villages. Kwikuba, one of the villages, was where one of the first Umoja process began. I arrived in Kwikuba in August 2011 to understand how Umoja works in the field. One of the questions to be explored was,

> *Is Umoja a traditional participatory process with Bible verses added to it to help involve the church?*

Peter Ngwili is AICT CCMP Coordinator. He has been mobilising churches using Umoja methodology in Tanzania for close to 10 years. He has trained over 20 community facilitators across 15 villages. He responded to the question thus:

> *Umoja is about allowing poor communities to discover God's plans for their lives. It allows the poor to come together, dream big and explore resources they have from their surroundings to address poverty.*

The process not only deals with tangible resources, but harnesses 'softer' resources such as skills and attitudes in the community. Unlike most development approaches that have resulted in donor dependency, outside money and resources are used mainly for facilitation and only for inputs that are outside the capacities of the community. From the start communities understand that success largely rests on their own efforts.

In Kwikuba, the communities had constructed a ten-roomed health centre that met government quality regulations; a number of groups were formed dealing with issues such as HIV/AIDS, farming and village saving credit groups. Many of the groups had been formed ten years ago and were still functioning.

The diocese had conducted an assessment (Comprehensive Report for the Baseline Survey for the Community Self-help Groups Empowerment Programme) across the 15 villages where Umoja had been implemented. Apart from a clinic in Kwikuba, the village of Wagate had built a secondary school. A total of 176 groups were operational with 3,873 members directly involved and benefitting 20,000 people. All groups were involved in income generation and the assessment estimated capital of Tanzania shilling 203 million or USD 125,000.

The assessment did not include the value of community amenities such as schools and health clinics. The important point is that most of the work was from communities' own resources.

Working closely with Peter Ngwili is Sam. I met them in Kwikuba village. Sam proudly clutched his facilitator's bag that contained the Umoja facilitator's manual. He was born and raised in Kwikuba. He knows this community well and they know him. And he is trusted.

The role of the community CCMP facilitators is to take the community through the CCMP process, which often takes 1-2 years before tangible results can be seen – this is too slow for traditional development projects with three-year end dates. Sam explains the importance of going at the pace of the community: There is a saying in Swahili that,

If you want to go quickly go alone, if you want to go far let's walk together.

Many communities want to go far.

THE UMOJA PROCESS

1. To explain the Umoja process Sam took a stick, and drew a big circle in the dust. Marking clockwise on the circle, the first step is *church awakening*. At this stage, very experienced facilitators from

outside their community raise awareness in local church leaders about their congregation's responsibilities to the poor.
2. This is done through tailor-made Bible studies over several separate meetings. The main idea is to use a source that church leaders can identify with. Sam's favourite one is the story of Jesus feeding the 5,000. Jesus used resources in the community (the five loaves and two fish) and then multiplied them to feed the gathering crowd. Jesus did not come with his own baskets of food. The story goes straight to the heart of Umoja. Many church leaders, including the most sceptical, take note.
3. Once church leaders and congregation understand what Umoja is all about and indicate willingness to proceed, individuals are selected as community facilitators. They go through extensive training in the science and art of facilitation – by more experienced facilitators such as Peter Ngwili. After that, the church is ready to interact with the community.

Peter interjected saying it is similar to the security announcements before an airplane takes off: "Only once your oxygen is securely fastened should you help fellow passengers." Only when the church has understood, is totally committed, and has potentially skilled facilitators, can it go out to help the rest of the community. Then the community can take off. It would be disastrous for a church that is half committed and unprepared to the process to engage community time.

4. The next series of steps involves the rest of the community. Men and women, young and old, are brought together. Through a series of facilitated meetings, participatory tools are used to help communities understand the poverty in their area, identify the most vulnerable and reflect on their history to explore why and how they found themselves in this situation.

Sometimes when tracing their history the community may challenge some deeply held beliefs. In one case, the community discovered that the inheritance practices that saw widows losing their property were not as deep-rooted as was perceived in the community. They could trace the practice to a few decades rather than hundreds of years. Somehow a practice that for a century had been designed as a good safety net for widows and children had, due to growing greed, become a burden for grieving women and children. Such self-reflection that Umoja offers makes it more likely for the community to build up the confidence and motivation to change. An outsider would have had more difficulties.

The steps of Umoja are easy to understand. But Umoja is more of an art than a science. The facilitator needs to be highly skilled. She has to be able to help a diverse community overcome cultural practices such as women not being allowed to speak in front of men, and ensure that illiterate members are not lost in the discussions. Harmful and yet deep-rooted beliefs and practices have to be approached sensitively.

It is also a political process. It brings together disadvantaged groups, local churches and communities to change lives and the status quo. Not everyone is happy that previously powerless individuals, spouses or groups are now gaining strength and confidence. The potential for tensions either within the group or from outside is always present – tension that if not facilitated carefully can derail the whole process, especially in very conservative communities.

In different contexts, communities come up with different interventions. In some they decided that provision of safe and portable water was important, for others it was education. In another remote AICT diocese close to the Rwandan border, the community decided to build a police station as thefts were on the increase. However, certain results of Umoja are consistent. The communities became more resourceful and developed a more 'can do' attitude. Umoja also provided a safe space for different people in the community to be involved and have a say. This is important in contexts where the price for different voices being expressed is often dismissal or violence.

THE INFLUENCE AND EXPANSION OF UMOJA

The impact of Umoja has resulted in more Christian organisations having a second or closer look at working with local churches. For example, Tearfund now supports Umoja through the Council of Anglican Provinces in Africa. Through Tearfund's local partners in Tanzania, a church-planting organisation from the USA has started rolling out Umoja. Tearfund has recently helped create a loose network of 'Friends of Umoja' that bring together different organisations and individuals globally interested in promoting this practice.

More recently some secular organisations have also demonstrated willingness to have a fresh look at the work of the church, and in a few cases have provided grants through local churches. In 2009 I met one such organisation whilst on an official visit to Mozambique.

Tearfund's country representative for Mozambique organised a meeting with a leading Scandinavian donor agency in the capital Maputo. The purpose of the meeting was, amongst others, to persuade the organisation to consider supporting local churches. The official we met explained to us that his organisation's funding policies did not allow him to fund Christian organisations or churches. The tables had been turned. I was on the other side of the discussion – explaining the value of working with the local church.

What pleasantly surprised us was that on at least one occasion, despite their policy the donor agency had agreed to fund a development initiative of an Anglican Diocese to the north of Mozambique. They were impressed by the quality of the church work and their understanding of the local context.

We did not obtain any specific funding leads. However, we left with some useful advice. He said that in the end, all donors whether secular or not, want their resources to be associated with what works. If churches can provide more evidence of sound development impact and sustainability – more secular organisations will be willing to work with them.

PRINCIPLES OF UMOJA

Sustainability

Not about sustaining projects, but sustaining passion to solve own problems.

When development experts look for signs of sustainability, the focus is mostly on whether activities that were funded have continued after the funding has ceased. With Umoja the focus is not so much on sustaining project activities, but on sustaining a community's passion to continue to solve their own problems. Today the main problem may be lack of water – but in a couple of decades the community may be confronting a totally different problem. The idea is that they can draw on the experience of solving the water problem to solve even bigger problems. To achieve that experience, the community has to be involved in-depth.

As part of the sustainability question, development experts also ask when their job is done. It is clear that even when a development initiative has improved say the health or welfare of the poor, it can not guarantee that the same people will not fall into hard times in the future. One lesson from the global economic downturn of 2009 is that no community, even in the west, is eternally immune from a lean season.

Probably the job of external development agencies is done when development efforts create support structures that are permanently present to help the poor to step out of poverty, or to provide a buffer should they fall on hard times. The local churches provide that permanent presence before, during and after external support to development initiatives have ceased. Through Umoja the idea is to proactively and deliberately utilise the local church as one of key community resource.

Ownership

To ensure sustainability, ownership is another key aspect that focuses the attention of those designing development projects. This is a key principle of Umoja.

My first lesson in community ownership was under a tree in the Dotito village, Zimbabwe. A community meeting had been hastily arranged to deal with a problem of a growing number of people in the community who were violating agreed rules around fishing. The programme I managed had constructed a medium-sized dam to help irrigation, provide water for livestock and which was stocked with fish. One rule for fishing was that everyone who fished had to pay a certain amount for a day's fishing. Some people who fished refused to pay because they had not caught anything. They may have felt justified, but the rules had been agreed by all.

In addition, some community members had started planting too close to the dam – causing soil erosion and silt filling the dam. This threatened to cut the lifespan of the dam by half.

The meeting under a mango tree was the fourth one and still there had been no agreement. I felt we were not getting anywhere amidst all the accusations. My team and I reminded the gathering that the dam was owned by the community and it was their responsibility to take care of it.

Eventually, an elderly man stood up and said he found it strange that a meeting had to be called more than three times to convince the community they owned the dam. He pointed his walking stick to some cows a distance away. He said those cows were his. He does not need anyone to remind him of this. "What sort of ownership is this?" he added, before spitting on the ground to emphasise the seriousness of his point (rather than in disgust), before sitting down.

The difference of course was the old man paid for his cows, and in the case of the development programme the money was provided. Even though the community contributed labour, our contribution had been significant.

The lessons from the Umoja process show that stronger ownership is achieved when communities are given the chance to contribute to the bulk of any initiative. It is even better when that contribution from the community is financial.

But the communities are often poor. Can they contribute financially? My experience is that if you find a beer hall or pub in a poor community, it is a sign that there is some money circulating – it just needs to be channelled for good causes. Umoja has managed to divert some of these financial resources, partly by managing expectations from the start of the process.

In an Umoja awareness video, Tearfund's representative for Tanzania, Justin Nyamonga, explained that with traditional projects money from outside is provided. These projects usually have a definite time frame – usually three years. Members of the community have grown to understand that once the money runs out or it is the end of the project, the activities stop.

With Umoja from the start there is an emphasis that no money is provided. In addition, Umoja is a process rather than a project with a definite end date. To the frustration of some, Umoja can not be placed neatly into common time bound planning tools such as 'log frames'.

OUTSTANDING ISSUES

Raising funds for Umoja

Questions that Tearfund's marketing team have been asking of Umoja are:

How do you raise funds to support a process when many people want to give money to tangible projects? How do you support initiatives where tangible results may only emerge after two years?

Umoja makes good development sense, but is difficult to fundraise for. There are questions regarding on what basis Tearfund supporters should give if communities are becoming self sufficient?

Part of the answer is that not all communities have reached a stage of self-sufficiency where they do not need additional help. There are still more communities that would benefit from an expansion of this work. The other part is that in areas where Umoja is working well, it does not mean that communities have all the skills and resources to deal with all the problems. External assistance is still welcome. For example, at the clinics and schools that communities built in Kwikuba and Wagate, the government provided the nurses and teachers. What Umoja contributes is the notion that external assistance is provided in line with communities' priorities and an understanding that its success largely depends on the communities themselves.

Bringing churches to work together

Umoja is a Swahili name for being of the same mind. Many people outside the church are often surprised that churches do not always work together. Umoja – the process – brings different local churches together to help their community. But it is not easy in any environment – as one young community organiser found.

In 1985, a young community volunteer worked for an organisation called Development Communities Project (DCP). It was set up by Reverend Kelly, a white minister. DCP was set up to mobilise churches to address the problems in the aftermath of steel plant closures in the south side of Chicago, USA. Part of DCP's work was to set up drugs and after-school programmes for the unemployed and youth who were mainly black.

The community organiser met Pastor Charles Smalls inviting his church to join the DCP campaign. In between sipping his coffee and looking at the flyer from DCP, Pastor Smalls dismissed the young community organiser: "…the last thing we need is to join up with white money and Catholic churches and Jewish organisers to solve our problems." (Barack Obama, *Dreams of My Father* [Canongate Books, 2007], 261).

Sustainable Development, Through Mobilising Churches

Years later the not-so young man was nicknamed 'community organiser-in-chief'. He had learnt not only about the challenges of bringing local churches together to one cause. He also learnt the power of community organising or mobilisation. His name was Barack Obama who used this experience to become the first black President of the USA in November 2008, and again in 2012.

Not all community organisers become high profile like President Obama. But many share the experience that it is not a given that churches of different denominations will want to work together, even if the cause is worthwhile. Sometimes unfortunately the local church acts as a thermometer, reflecting the divisions within a society. The Umoja process is about helping the local church and community to be a thermostat – setting pace for new relations amongst different churches and within the community that helps overcome poverty.

Working through contentious issues

It is important to recognise that the church is not homogenous. This was a constant reminder for members of a working group set up in the UK to develop partnership principles to help provide a platform for cooperation between DFID and faith groups and by extension the church. The working group was set up by the former Secretary for International Development, Andrew Mitchell, in January 2011. I was one of its members.

The working group produced partnership principles that underscored the need for finding a common ground between secular and faith groups. The common ground for partnering with faith groups found was poverty alleviation. The paper also recognised that there are contentious issues where secular world and faith groups, including the church are unlikely to agree. However, the spirit of cooperation needed to start from where both sides could agree rather than start from where the disagreement were.

When the partnership principles were launched in 2012, Mr Andrew Mitchell remarked that,

Faith plays a vital role in development. Faith groups are often the first place poor people turn in times of need. They are a source of compassion, generosity and succour to many in the developing world. (Source DFID, June 2012)

Church losing it identity
Curiously the biggest hesitation of the local church to be involved in community development comes from the church itself. Some church leaders feel that it is not the business of the church to be involved in community development. Other leaders who see a role for the church are concerned that the secular world demands that it helps the poor as an NGO by, for example, down-playing its spiritual work.

Views from the community
It seems appropriate that the last word about the role of the church comes from people who benefitted directly from the work of the church – the poor themselves.

> *Machan Diraguti is from Wagete Village in Tanzania:*
>
> *Cladding a yellow baseball cap and pale blue shirt he explained the beginnings of Umoja. At the start when Machan realised that Umoja was not about external money coming to the village he asked Umoja coordinators, "What have you brought for us, just words and stories?"*
>
> *He then explained, "Slowly (as the process progressed) we began to realise we had a responsibility. Development was dependent on us. When we discovered that we declared war on poverty. We are still fighting poverty today. We used to go far away for water and share the source with animals and baboons. We used to experience bilharzia and diarrhoea. Now we have clean water in our village. The (Umoja) process has opened our eyes. We feel the difference."*
>
> *Lucy Kasmiro is also from Wagete Village:*
>
> *As women we were in a very terrible situation. But we realised that, even as women, we had resources to change our situations. The (Umoja) sessions involving women and men taught us that we can participate equally. Relations between husband and wives have improved – because the sense of working together is happening at family level as well. As a result we no longer farm with a child on our backs and dig the soil by hand. Instead we are now using oxen and the work is much less strenuous. 'This is all by the grace of God'.*
>
> *Elena Chamba, volunteer Community Resource Person from Kwikuba Village in Tanzania:*

Sustainable Development, Through Mobilising Churches

Elena is also part of a small group focusing on farming and savings and credit. She helps train community members on effective farming approaches.

"Firstly I want to thank the church so much for bringing our community together and make us unite."

"Through the savings and credit group and a grain grinding income generating project I was able to take my child to secondary school. This child is now finishing secondary school. I feel proud that my child is finishing education. I now also have two other children in secondary school."

LISTENING TO THE POOR, IN MICROFINANCE

IRENE MUTALIMA

Irene Banda Mutalima is the Founder and CEO of TUCUZA Associates Limited focusing on transformative entrepreneurship. She was previously Executive Director of ECLOF International, African Regional Co-ordinator for Opportunity International, Consultant to DFID, and a founding member of CETZAM.

'Africa Rising!' was the title of the December 2011 edition of the Economist magazine announcing the good news coming out of Africa. The magazine cited Africa as having six of the ten fastest growing countries with at least a quarter of revenues coming from natural resources like copper, oil and gold. Eleven years earlier, the same magazine produced their May 2000 edition with the title 'Hopeless Continent' showing an image of Africa with the picture of a man wielding a weapon of sorts against a black background. This edition highlighted African as beset with all manner of problems at a large scale: disease especially in the wake of HIV/AIDS, wars, famine, floods, drought, etc. Indeed there is now good news coming out of Africa.

'Hopeless Continent' seemed like a terrible indictment on Africa. The Churches Commission for England and Ireland decided to send a team that would offer a response while engaging with development agencies at a briefing in London. I was asked to be part of that team. At the time, I was in Oxford, just starting my own journey of academic reflection on the very issues of poverty and squalor. This journey was also in response to Africa's woes, and joined the many efforts that are now producing good news out of Africa.

Years earlier, I had joined hands with colleagues in Zambia who were equally concerned with the high levels of poverty and with the fact that able-bodied men simply had no jobs and therefore could not look after their families. High levels of unemployment had thrown people into the informal marketplace where they struggled to eke out a living. Women had also taken the role of provider and did petty trading at any space that would be available: a table right by the street in their front yard or a stall at the open market. Our ruminations about this state of affairs led to the establishment of a microfinance institution called CETZAM, with the help of Opportunity International and funding provided by DFID. The microfinance institution, CETZAM, would provide much-needed finance to improve business incomes and improve people's lives.

AFRICA'S WOES

There is no question about Africa having lagged behind in development compared to other continents. Low rates of industrialisation resulted in low economic advancement. In seeking solutions, the development agenda initially sought solutions that would improve economic growth at country level. It was however observed that one of the undesirable offshoots of low economic growth was increasing levels of poverty and diminishing prospects for poor people. Thus the development focus shifted to include a high focus on human development.

THE HUMAN DEVELOPMENT PERSPECTIVE

The Human Development approach was espoused on the premise of enlarging people's choices and enhancing human capabilities and freedoms to enable them to enjoy long, healthy and creative lives. Human deprivation was seen as a lack of basic needs like food, shelter and health services. Using this basic needs understanding as a starting point, the Human Development approach aimed to remove the focus from national economic prosperity and bring it to people who experienced the reality of life. Thus experts developed indicators to help nations track improvements in the critical areas of human endeavour such as:

- ability to live long and healthy lives
- life expectancy at birth
- being able to acquire knowledge and skills
- gender inequalities
- decent standards of living.

At a more basic level, food insecurity became rampant in developing countries calling for remedial actions. The 1974 World Food Conference to discuss the food crisis, endorsed the resolution that each, man, woman or child has the "inalienable right to be free from hunger and malnutrition in order to develop their physical and mental faculties." The fulfilment of this resolution triggered massive advances in technology leading to significant improvements in agricultural yields in developed nations. International organisations funded research for transfer and adaptation of agricultural systems and technologies to developing countries. These technological advances produced phenomenal growth in agricultural yields and the process became known as the Green Revolution.

However, Africa did not benefit much from the success of the Green Revolution. Poor infrastructure, high transport costs, limited investment in irrigation, and pricing and marketing policies that penalised farmers made the Green Revolution technologies too expensive or inappropriate for much of Africa. The food crisis in Africa of the 1980s revealed that at household level, food insecurity was rampant even when supply at national level was assured. This was manifesting in increased incidences of famine, hunger and malnutrition. Solutions to ensure household food security were sought.

Not surprisingly, surveys revealed that people living in poverty were already active in entrepreneurial activities to support livelihoods. The International Labour Organisation (ILO) championed the cause of these entrepreneurs and in 1972 coined the term 'informal sector' to denote the space that was serving the employment needs of small and micro enterprises. By the 1980s the informal sector had developed very rapidly in developing countries and was considered the right space for development thinking and funding, mostly through NGOs. One of the important observations was that the entrepreneurs had minimal or no access to formal credit services to finance their businesses. This was the niche that microfinance stepped into.

A STRATEGY FOR POVERTY REDUCTION

Microfinance has its focus on developing poor people. As MicroFinance Institutions (MFIs) expand they becoe available in areas where poor people are located and create critical infrastructure necessary for deploying financial services that respond to the needs of poor. Thus microfinance moves the development focus from hand-outs and welfare support, to empowering poor people to help themselves.

Africa has about 320 million people living on less than $1 a day. Yet, there is less than 3% penetration of financial services. Because of low employment, African economies have large informal sectors where people have the potential to grow their businesses. Both these factors define the space that microfinance can penetrate and expand in order to bring good news for Africa.

However, Africa presents unique challenges that hinder exponential growth of the microfinance industry. Microfinance does not do well in areas of low population density and low GDP per capita. Delivering financial services benefits from economies of scale where there is high population density. Low GDP per capita implies small transactions whose profitability comes in equally minuscule doses. Thus the combination of high cost of service delivery and low earnings on those services does not make the microfinance proposition in Africa that appealing. Yet, in spite of these major challenges in Africa, success stories are becoming evident.

At the end of 2008 MFIs in Sub-Saharan Africa were reaching 6.5 million borrowers and 16.5 million savers representing a penetration rate of 3% for borrowers and 5% for savers. This growth represented more borrowers than in Eastern Europe and Central Asia, the Middle East and North Africa. In terms of depositors, SSA reflects the highest growth of the microfinance industry at 40% over the previous year. These deposits provided up to 60% of the funding needed for loans. This means that a large portion of the lending portfolio was supported by local funds. MFIs in SSA are also innovating for the benefit of poor people. Up to 28 countries embarked on branchless banking with a focus on payments and transfers using mobile phone services.

SOME PERSONAL STORIES

At home, we had our own programme CETZAM (Christian Enterprise Trust, Zambia). Giving our clients access to small amounts of credit enabled them to increase their volumes of trade and thus increase their family incomes. Our loans started from a very small amount of the equivalent of US$20.00 and were often payable over a period of four months. These small loans were a source of good news. Clients told us that their children were having better meals, going back to school because fees had been paid, and were able to seek better medical attention as a result of improved incomes.

> *A member of one group in Kitwe got to her home, only to find that her son had sustained a fractured limb from a fall. Group members quickly gathered to offer support. The child needed to be taken to hospital and money would be needed for the taxi as well as to pay for medical attention. Immediately group members*

Listening to the Poor, in MicroFinance

realised that unless they pitched in, the loan that had been given to this member would be used towards this emergency and the business would suffer. So they agreed to contribute their own money towards the emergency. They also took the loan money for safekeeping until their colleague was past the crisis and was able to do business again.

This experience made them realise the importance of having their own group savings to meet emergency needs so that they would not disturb the business. One of the factors that have been cited for short business cycles among poor people is that they experience many shocks that then have a claim on the meagre resources. This experience enabled us to see the need for further buffers against shocks, and therefore early conversations regarding micro-insurance started with this group in Kitwe. Micro-insurance is now a global offering.

A client in Mufulira town had borrowed to improve his bicycle mending business. He managed his loan very well and his business thrived. This not only improved his family income, but also gave him increased self-esteem. Unfortunately he succumbed to illness, and died. The family experienced a sense of loss including the impending loss of income. The good news though is that his teenage son stepped up and offered to take over the business. He managed the business well and grew it even beyond what his father had done. When asked how he managed, he proudly mentioned that his father had taught him the business and that he would continue looking after the family.

At another group meeting, a male client proudly stood up to the applause of the rest of the group. The sense of camaraderie suggested events whose stories were waiting to be told. The client's story was that he had been without a job for such a long time that his own family stopped looking to him for anything. He became the laughing-stock of the community. Then CETZAM came to his area. Some friends encouraged him to start a business mending shoes. The good news of this story is that at the time of my visit, his business was doing quite well, and he had started contributing to the family welfare again. It was no longer unusual to see him walk out of the market with a chicken that he would have bought for his family from his earnings. And so the good news was that now when he stood up to speak, people had to listen. He had finally come into his own, as a result of a small loan.

A group living in squalor on swampy grounds on the outskirts of a small town close to the Zambia/Congo DRC Border could no longer live with the poverty that surrounded them. They approached our office for a small loan to purchase vegetable seeds for a garden. They transformed the swampy area into a very productive place where they grew a variety of vegetables. Each morning, they took turns transporting the vegetables to the local market for sale and they shared the money. Not only did they improve their lives, but also transforming the swampy land reduced the incidences of mosquitoes, which cause malaria.

An assessment study done on our CETZAM programme in 2000 reported:

Usefulness of the loan
Clients used CETZAM loans to purchase stock in bulk or diversify product range. They also invested more in tools and equipment for business development, and on improving their premises. They related changes in household income to business income rather than receipts from other household members. They also spent significantly on household improvements and on household assets. Clients felt they had become better at business, more disciplined with money and worked harder.

Impact on household welfare
Three quarters of the respondents (73.3%) reported an improvement in their food consumption. They no longer went to bed hungry and were able to feed their families better. Less than half of the sampled number (48.3%) was able to purchase new assets for their household and these range from kitchen dresser, plates and pans, sofas, a bicycle, black and white television, etc. ... A number of clients reported being able through loan profits to provide for school needs of members of the family and to clothe themselves.

Perceptual impact
Respondents are reported to have perceived themselves as having changed for the better... they had gained self-esteem, self-confidence and a vision for the future... increased wealth. Clients who were also members of the loan group felt a sense of belonging and inter-dependency and not being the ones begging. Clients were better able to handle shocks as they had access to money and could meet unforeseen needs (Copestake 2002).

THE IMPORTANCE OF SAVINGS TO POOR PEOPLE
Poor people need both savings and credit services. Poor people need to spend on lifecycle needs that include homebuilding, leaving an inheritance,

etc.; emergencies like injuries, floods, wars, fires or loss of homes, especially for those in squatter settlements; and to invest in opportunities like buying land or starting a business. These activities often require large sums of money which can best be accumulated over time, and so mostly poor people will either sell assets, get a loan or find ways of turning their small savings into useful larger lumps.

In 1991 CARE International started the village savings and loan associations (VSLA) in Niger built entirely on member savings using participatory community-based approaches. By 2008, VSLA programmes had been initiated in 21 countries. Following these positive results, CARE set up a project called Access Africa which will enable expansion of VSLA to 39 countries across Africa and reach 30 million poor people, 70% of whom will be women by 2018.

In a similar fashion, Catholic Relief Services (CRS) introduced the savings and lending communities (SILC) programme as an improvement of traditional savings methods. SILC enables members to:

- determine the minimum and maximum level of saving that each member would make. This enables the very poor to participate while accommodating those who might want to pay in more.
- provide flexible credit where members again determine the amounts they can access.
- And provide insurance for emergencies through a social fund that is paid in separately from savings.

By 2010, SILC operations had expanded to 27 African countries and was proliferating within those countries.

In CETZAM, due to regulatory conditions, we could not take any voluntary savings. However, we took savings as security for the loan. The savings were meant to be returned after the loan had been paid. We observed that most of our clients desired to keep the savings with us as they considered it a safe place. In order to accommodate this need, we opted to obtain a licence that would enable us to take those deposits.

LIMITS TO MICROFINANCE

Microfinance has attracted criticism around its efficacy as a development strategy. It has been described as a 'global fad' where poor people have to live with the stigma of debt. Critics note the inadequacy of microfinance for poor people whose needs include other services like health, schools, etc., and that targeting the entrepreneurial poor has excluded the very poor and the rural poor from microfinance programmes.

At home, I was more concerned with how we listened to poor people. As decision makers, we spent a lot of time in the management of the organisation and not necessarily listening and engaging poor people. I interviewed one Loan Officer to find out how she determined who was poor and needed our service. Her answer was that her selection criterion was not necessarily on the basis of the poverty status of the client but more on their capacity to repay the loan. She told me that her performance would not be judged by her capacity to serve more poor people but by the quality of her loan portfolio signified by the how good the repayments were. She therefore did not want to jeopardise her career by focusing on poor people who would give her trouble repaying the loan anyway. I realised that there was indeed a very thin line between managing the programme and ensuring that poor people were served.

One client described how she obtained a loan. Her neighbour approached her to be part of the group because they had fallen short of the number of people needed to get a loan. She did not need the loan but in order to help constitute a group, she joined and got her first loan. In our books, this loan performed well, but her narration was revealing. She told me that she used the same amount to repay the loan, and needed more to cover initial charges and interest payment. It was only in her second loan that she was able to start a business.

Discussions at group meetings were entirely around the group's capacity to repay their loans. Management interacted with poor people mostly to encourage prompt repayments. Faced with poor repayments in the programme, we instituted a study to find out from our client the reasons for defaults in payments. The finding indicated that poor people had views about the services we offered:

CETZAM Product Feature	Client response
Credit products have fixed repayment periods that are non-negotiable.	Generally clients favoured to obtain control over loan repayment methods and timing. They also wished that repayments would be structured in ways that would meet the changes in their businesses

Product requires that repayments start following week after obtaining a loan (this is for loans that are repayable on a weekly basis).	Some clients needed a grace period while others would have loved to make fortnightly payments and not weekly.
Product is based on mutual guarantee in place of tangible collateral. It is assumed that clients will empathise with one another and pay for the defaulters.	In a group, members were not willing to assist members who were having difficulties. Clients felt that CETZAM should deal with clients who fail to pay.
Product assumes that group will make proper assessment of business capacity to service loan before it is given.	Poor business planning as reason for business failure. Clients did not have the expertise to assess the potential of businesses.
Product feature has minimum of 25 and maximum 40 members for cost effectiveness.	Groups of 25 too big and therefore difficult to ensure cohesion.
Product insists on women leadership as it has been 'proven' that they are more accommodating.	Some groups are happy to have men as their leaders.

The findings echoed similar findings by a World Bank study to understand the perspectives of poor people. That study acknowledged that poor people's views are not always considered when crafting development solutions that will affect them. The study made an observation that 'there are 2.8 billion poverty experts, the poor themselves. Yet the development discourse about poverty has been dominated by the perspectives and expertise of those who are not poor - professionals, politicians and agency officials.'

The following concerns are indicative of possible exclusion of poor people's views:
- The entry of profit-driven investors in the industry has engendered the drive for profits in microfinance thereby inadvertently excluding the ultra-poor whose status renders them more risky to be included as microfinance clients.
- The proliferation of microfinance institutions has resulted in multiple borrowing among poor people, thereby exposing them to greater indebtedness. Additionally it is argued that interest rates charged tend to become usurious.

- With the depressed levels of financial education among poor people, they are unable to make meaningful contributions to the design of financial services that will enable sustainable economic growth.
- Connected to the above issue is the concern that continued service to the micro-entrepreneurs can only be at the expense of small and medium-sized entrepreneurs who have the potential for growth leading employment creation and therefore adding to a country's economic growth.

A Typical Microfinance Institution

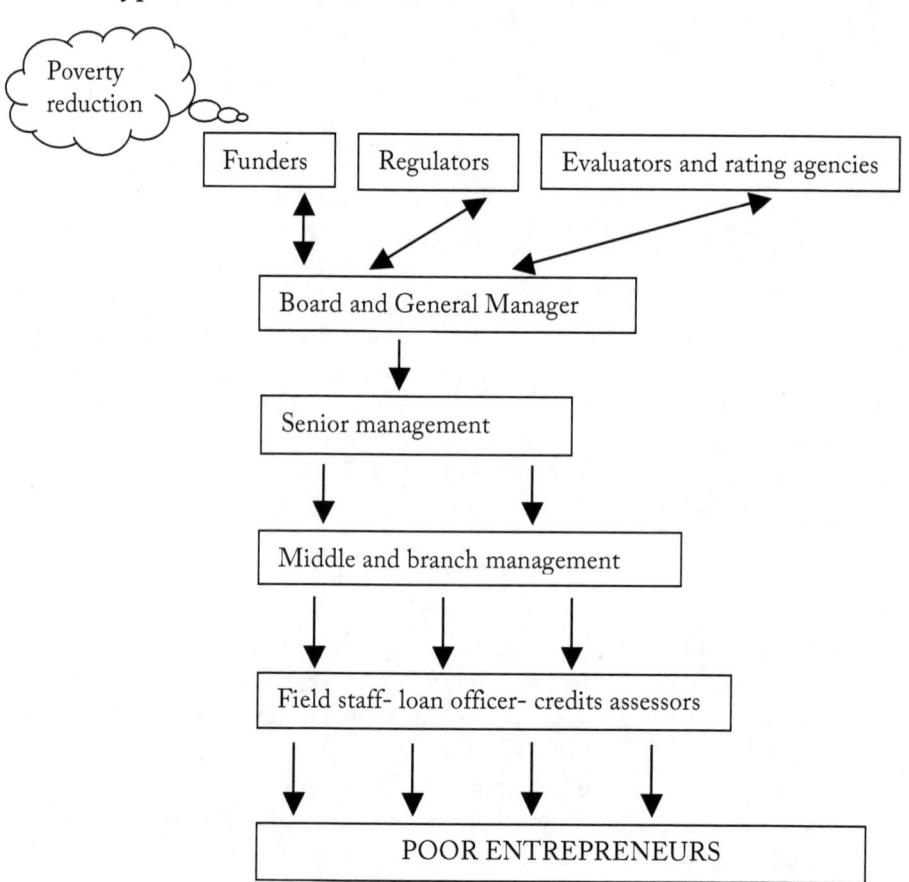

```
         (Poverty reduction)

    Funders    Regulators    Evaluators and rating agencies
                   │
         Board and General Manager
                   │
            Senior management
                   │
         Middle and branch management
                   │
      Field staff- loan officer- credits assessors
                   │
              POOR ENTREPRENEURS
```

THE VOICES IN MICROFINANCE

MFI TENSIONS
Which voice is important?
- Funder can stop money flow
- Regulator can shut us down
- Evaluator can represent us poorly
- Poor client very important for mission

THE VALUES
- Respect for the poor
- Listen to them and serve them well
- Learn from them
- Engage socially in enriching ways
- wholistic transformation

Poor entrepreneur
- get loan and pay back in time
- find market and improve business
- Observe conditions of loan

Microfinance Institutions

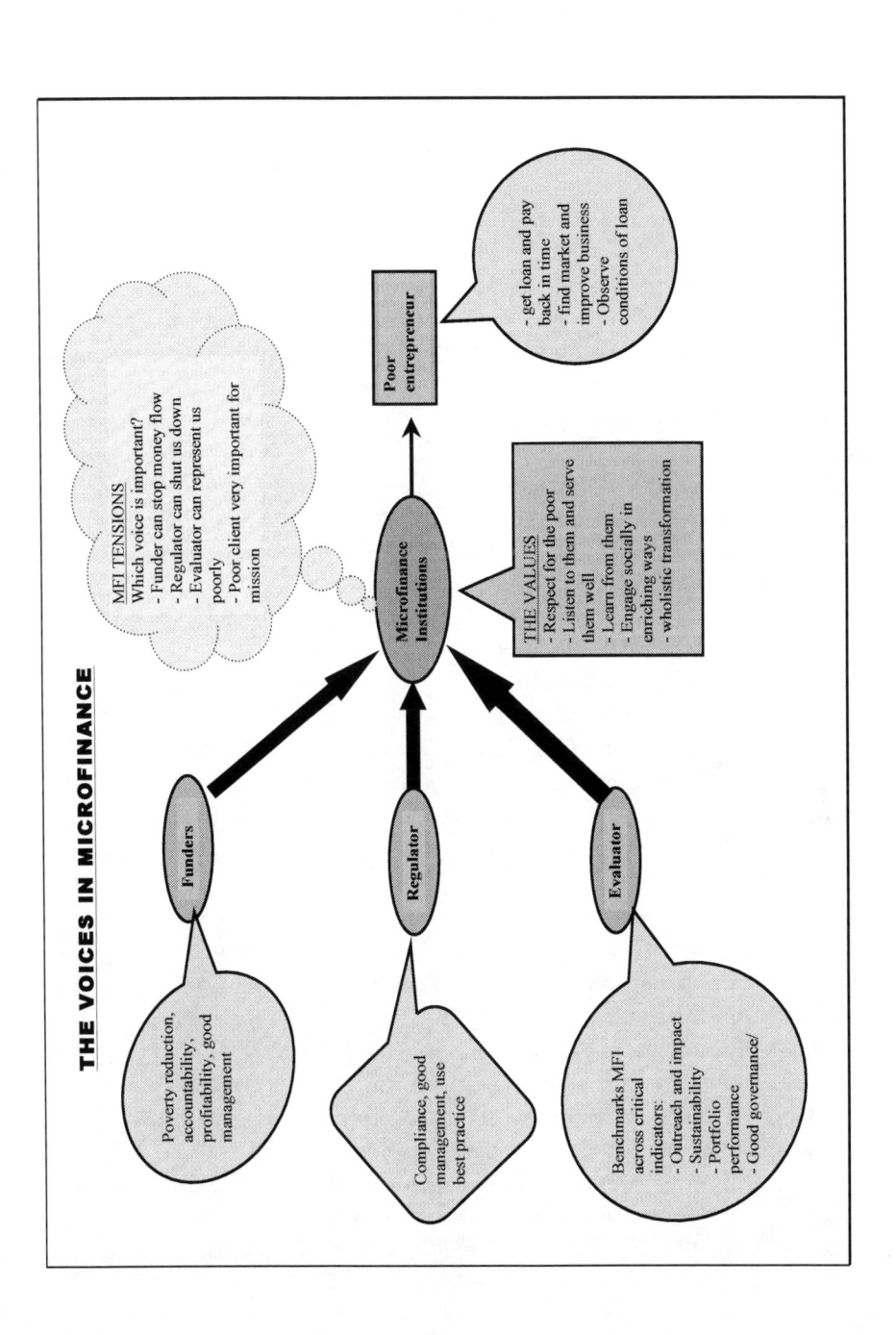

Funders — Poverty reduction, accountability, profitability, good management

Regulator — Compliance, good management, use best practice

Evaluator — Benchmarks MFI across critical indicators:
- Outreach and impact
- Sustainability
- Portfolio performance
- Good governance/

It is evident that in the provision of microfinance, those in the realm of the technical, political and social milieu influence the processes and methods. More importantly, it is those with resources whose voice tends to be favoured. In line with the World Bank assertion that poor people should be allowed a voice, the question is: how much of a voice can poor people have to influence decisions in microfinance when they do not hold the means to do so?

The diagrammatic representations (previous pages) attempt to capture the multi-layered structure of a typical microfinance institution and some of the competing voices that create tension and probably alienate poor people further. (At each level some of the resources and energy are dissipated, and a small proportion of the donors gifts actually get down to the poor!)

In this tension-laden environment, the intention to serve poor people is inherent. However the system has the potential of being an impediment to listening to poor people. Serving the system almost supersedes serving poor people.

SOLUTIONS TO IDENTIFIED PROBLEMS

In response to such concerns, microfinance institutions are now compelled to demonstrate the impact of their programmes on the lives of poor people over and above the health of the organisations. Other campaigns are focused on ensuring that microfinance institutions abide by principles that safeguard the interests of microfinance clients from potentially harmful financial products, through appropriate policies, practices, and products, and ensure that they are treated fairly.

Africa has high levels of financial illiteracy and financial exclusion. This means inability to plan, budget and invest. It also means the inability to know where to get information on financial services, understand what is on offer and the cost of accessing the services. To address this situation, national and international institutions are financing education to improve financial knowledge and skills, raising awareness of financial issues and improving financial access. The targeted populations are largely low-income and vulnerable people, women and youths.

These initiatives are critical to engaging poor people and enabling them to give a voice that will truly contribute to their welfare.

The role of the church
The church has many strategic advantages in poverty alleviation in Africa:
- It is rooted in the community, in rural and urban areas including in areas of conflict. It draws its voluntary membership from local population; therefore it is the locus of local knowledge.
- It is non-partisan, serving the whole society, family, community, and government, rich and poor people alike.
- It offers stability with minimum disruptions, unlike NGOs or governments, which would be disrupted by unstable funding possibilities and elections vagaries.
- The traditional African awe of religion means that the church is held in high esteem and therefore commands a high level of influence and can be the representative voice of poor people.
- It has a long and established history of socio-economic development work that has benefited needy people.
- The church also has existing structures and mechanisms to initiate and maintain new activities.

Given this advantageous position, the church needs to engage in the initiatives to empower poor people and enable their voices. The development of SILC through Catholic Relief Services is one of those critical engagements that open up space for poor people.

LISTENING TO THE POOR IN CHIPATA COMPOUND OF LUSAKA
In a research survey to listen to poor people, the author engaged sixteen women in a squatter settlement in Lusaka, Zambia. The women are part of a community-driven co-operative society that was started under the auspices of CARE International to provide microfinance services. The research aims to understand among other things, how and whether poor people's stories of poverty have informed the design and delivery of financial services. Exploring various themes, the responses were telling.

When asked why they joined the group one respondent echoed the rest of the group members:

"We joined the group in order to learn and find wisdom." She proceeded to lament that their lives had not improved from being members of the co-operative. It was evident that a number of researchers had been to visit this group to understand their operations. This had left them with unfulfilled expectations. "People just come to learn from us and are not interested in our welfare. They learn from us. After learning from what is going on in our compound, they leave and never come back. No one seems to be interested in helping us move forward."

When asked about what they wanted to learn, the respondents showed concerns about their knowledge of running businesses. "Please help us. Some of us have school-going children who have stopped because we have no money. We are strong and want to work, but we have not found someone committed to help us. No one has taught us how to do business. We cannot just start, someone needs to teach us, but there is no one to help us. We have remained behind. The groups are there but there is no one to help us move forward."

Given the admission that they did not have a good understanding of how to do business, they were asked why they still needed a loan. "These loans are given even when we have not asked for them. People come and tell us to form groups so we can get loans. When you do not have a business, the money is used in the home. That is how some people here get the money. Not many of us in this group have taken a loan. The co-operative does not have money to give us."

CONCLUSIONS, LESSONS LEARNED AND OUTSTANDING ISSUES

Microfinance has scored significant successes in Africa. The work is ongoing to ensure that poor people are given appropriate services that meet their needs and respond to moving them out of poverty. Critical to this ideal is the realisation that, in spite of the successes, financial inclusion in Africa has only attained a penetration rate of 3%. This is a real concern in light of the assumption that financial inclusion is key to poverty reduction, and that people participation is equally important for sustainable development. This being so, poor people can no longer remain passive beneficiaries.

Various initiatives have opened up opportunities for poor people to engage in the discourse of financial inclusion. However, engagement will not be meaningful unless poor people acquire the necessary knowledge to navigate the financial landscape. Though a lot of initiatives are in place, there is still more work to be done in some African countries. So the big outstanding issue is about how poor people can access the available knowledge, and empower themselves to start articulating their needs intelligently.

The church, as the existing structure where poor people are in Africa, needs to position itself to engage with the identified initiatives for the benefit of poor people. The church can champion the cause of ensuring financial literacy that will lead to sustainable development for poor people. The church can facilitate the emergence of a new financial narrative in Africa and this will enable poor people to engage more meaningfully in defining financial services that work for them.

ENGAGING WITH THE COMMUNITY, THE FIGHT AGAINST AIDS

JOSHUA BANDA

Bishop Joshua Banda is Senior Pastor of Northmead AOG Church, Zambia, President of the Southern Africa Region of the Pentecostal Assemblies of Africa, and Board Chairman, National AIDS Council-Zambia.

In 1992, while heading the Trans-Africa Theological College, I was invited to be one of the keynote presenters at a conference engaged in advocacy for human rights and good governance. The meeting was organised for key national and community leaders. The topic of the paper I was requested to deliver was 'The role of the church in crime preventions', not a subject I was an expert in. However, I was determined to seize the opportunity as a learning curve.

As I set out to search for what could be identified as the church's contribution to this area of crime prevention, it became abundantly clear that this was uncharted territory. So I turned to the Lord in prayer for fresh ideas and guidance, and was very encouraged when a plan began to unfold.

The plan involved carrying out a survey, through interviews, with key persons in the Zambian Police. My first interview was with a senior officer by the name of Francis Musonda. I was shocked to learn from him that up until this point, there was no history of the church's engagement in crime prevention initiatives. However, it was heartening to learn that the Zambian Police were actually looking for ways to collaborate with churches. Mr Musonda explained that he saw the church as a 'sleeping giant'. The church was, in his opinion, the most credible entity for anyone to partner with, for effective community service.

The simple truth came with such power and freshness that I was inspired to anchor the entire paper on it. Therefore, composing and delivering the paper at the conference became a turning point in my understanding of how imperative it was for the church to engage, both spiritually and socially, with community.

I argued in the paper that the mandate of the Lord Jesus Christ was for the church to be 'salt' and 'light' (Matthew 5:10-13) in a world that was faced with various forms of decay and darkness. In specific regard to crime preventions, I suggested practical steps such as the need to raise individual levels of awareness about crime prevention strategies, through tailor made civic education programmes. Further, that apart from reaching prisoners during their incarceration, the church could establish 'half-way houses' for rehabilitating past offenders, following their release from prison.

I concluded that the strategies for prevention of crime were adaptable and therefore could extend to the prevention of diseases, including HIV/AIDS, which was already at epidemic proportions. This process enriched my advocacy so much so that the next two decades marked defining levels of my personal engagement in the fight against HIV/AIDS.

RE-TRACING THE CHURCH'S INVOLVEMENT IN AIDS WORK IN ZAMBIA

As in most affected countries, AIDS work in Zambia traces its beginnings in the health sector. The Zambian church's involvement obviously predates HIV/AIDS work, since its health interventions go as far back as the early 1800s.

The church efforts in the sector are attributable initially, to the Churches Health Association of Zambia (CHAZ). Currently, the church's coverage in this respect represents approximately 35% of Zambia's total general healthcare provision, and over 50% of Zambia's rural healthcare provision.

There are three distinct phases to the progression of the church, in relation to HIV/AIDS. (1) The early days (1984-1990), when issues like HIV/AIDS were avoided on the pretext that they were purely medical and had little relevance to the spiritual mandate of the church; (2) the awakening of a latent conscience (1991-2000); and (3) the constructive engagement of church congregations (2001 to the present), when a greater level of the understanding that the gospel was holistic (caring for both body and spirit) was accepted. A number of church congregations, including our own (Northmead Assembly), now demonstrate in more ways than one that evangelism and social action should not be separated.

As sporadic church-based initiatives involving the church congregations themselves emerged, it became clear that a mechanism was needed to coordinate these noble efforts. It was undeniable that there was a gap to be filled.

The Expanded Church Response (ECR) to HIV/AIDS was formed in 1999 to fill that gap. Working with Dr Helmut Reutter, and with the financial support of World Vision Zambia, we mobilised 220 church leaders to discuss the dire need for collective action to confront the HIV/AIDS pandemic. Part of the outcome was the formation of a Task Force (team) that I was privileged to chair. Later on, the ECR was registered (2003) as a legal trust, with the mission of coordinating faith-based AIDS responses.

Currently managing an annual budget in excess of US $1.5 million in 2013, the ECR has cumulatively built the capacity of hundreds of church leaders, congregations and over 94 Faith-Based Organisations (FBOs) and health facilities. This has resulted in the delivery of high quality care, support and treatment to more than 28,270 beneficiaries in five of Zambia's ten provinces.

The great advantage of ECR, which includes working with more than 16,000 individual churches and millions of potential volunteers, is its ability to harness this high volume of human resource, coupled with the ability to act through established infrastructure already existent throughout the churches. This is particularly effective in the rural areas, where NGOs, especially those spread over multiple countries, have considerable difficulty reaching.

Over time the ECR has managed to grow a highly qualified team with extensive experience and a history of successful grant management. What ECR has achieved since its inception is testimony to the strength, capacity and overall comparative advantage of the church as a key player in the AIDS fight, while delivering life-saving services and development, in a sustainable manner. The sustainability is anchored in the assured perpetuity that lies in local churches, as they are in the community for long term good.

In particular Northmead Assembly of God (NAOG) has implemented several AIDS interventions, three of which I share here, namely the Lazarus Project, Operation Paseli, and Circle of Hope Clinic. These 'models' are replicable even in locations where resources may be thought to be extremely scarce or limited, because the community always has something in hand.

THE LAZARUS PROJECT: PROVIDING HOLISTIC CARE TO ORPHANED AND VULNERABLE CHILDREN (OVCs), THEIR FAMILIES AND COMMUNITIES

The Lazarus Project was founded in 1999 through an initiative that began as a feeding programme conducted by my wife, Pastor Gladys, and the women of the church. This was targeted initially towards children living on the streets. The feeding sessions were coupled with teachings on various issues ranging from spiritual and moral teachings, personal hygiene to life-skills. It soon became evident that there was a need to offer the children more than just monthly activities and meals. The need was to rescue them from the streets and provide them with a wholesome environment, shelter, good nutrition, and education in order to secure their future. The first steps started with the rescue of six vulnerable children who were placed in a safe home.

The Lazarus Project adopted a three-pronged approach involving outreach, rehabilitation and re-integration. The aim was to offer an opportunity for children to receive transformation progressively through programs that included spiritual formation, literacy training, skills training (carpentry, agriculture, poultry rearing), primary school education and recreation.

Over the years, the Lazarus Project managed to secure its own residential facility on a spacious 40 acre farm, where over 70 former street children were safely sheltered at a time. Utilising a vigorous family search program, relatives to most of the rehabilitated children were traced. This enabled the children to be re-integrated into society.

By the end of 2005, nearly 50 children had been successfully re-integrated, while others were simultaneously placed in school. Enrolment into the residential facility is currently earmarked for phase-out, following the success of the re-integration programme, enabling children not to be separated from their home roots.

To date, nearly 1,000 orphaned and vulnerable children have undergone training, registering amazing stories of transformation.

Engaging with the Community, The Fight Against AIDS

> *One of the most outstanding graduates from the programme is now in his third year of medical school at Zambia's prime University Teaching Hospital, Ridgeway Campus. Another boy, who completed high school with distinctions in Sciences and Additional Mathematics, is also in his third year towards a bachelors degree in Accounting and Production Management studies at Zambia's Copperbelt University.*

From 2004, for a successive period of three years, the Lazarus boys recorded 100% pass rate for grade eight qualification examination classes, held at seventh grade, with two boys being ranked among the top two highest scoring students in their respective schools.

Following the phase out of the residential program, the Lazarus activities are now focused on operation of an on-site Community School, the Lazarus Project Christian Community School, which has 400 orphaned and/or vulnerable boys and girls, currently enrolled in primary school classes, running from grade 1-7 and staffed by a team of seven full-time teachers. There are plans to expand the school in order to cater for more vulnerable and disadvantaged children from the surrounding poor communities, to meet the rising demand for quality education.

Going forward, the vision of the project has expanded beyond rescue of street children to providing holistic care and support for Orphaned and Vulnerable Children (OVCs), their families and communities.

OPERATION PASELI: OUTREACH TO, AND REHABILITATION OF, COMMERCIAL SEX WORKERS

"Sorry to call you so early, Pastor… you won't believe what we have just seen," stuttered the voice to which I awoke one Saturday morning. It was clear this was no ordinary call.

The caller was our Youth Director at church. The youths had been praying all Friday night. Their prayer meeting had ended at 5:30am. As the young people were leaving the church premises, they were shocked to see two adults (a man and a women) having sex on the pavement by the roadside, barely 10 metres from the main church gate. "We are so shocked Pastor, we are not sure what to do!" exclaimed the young man.

He concluded the lady was a prostitute, since many young prostitutes often paraded the street near church. I encouraged the young leader to take heart and to know that what he and others had just witnessed was, in reality, a manifestation of some deep spiritual needs of our community – just as well they had come from a prayer meeting. They could now intensify prayer vigils even more.

The seriousness of the reported incidence became a very heavy burden upon my heart. I sought God for guidance in relation to what we as a church could do about this. A number of troubling questions besieged my mind as I turned to prayer: What was the real state of our witness as a church in this location? What difference, if any, were we making in the community, so far? How could we reconcile our mission with the rampancy of prostitution and other risky behaviours that had now become characteristic of the night incidents in the vicinity of the church?

The next day, during the main Sunday Service, I announced my conclusions:

- First, I narrated the 6.00am call and my subsequent encounter with the Lord in prayer.
- Second, that in the wake of this encounter, we would suspend our usual weekly evening services and instead go on the streets (in pairs or triplets), to talk to the commercial sex workers.
- I lamented that there was no way we could carry on enjoying worship and payer in the four walls of the church while the community around us lay in moral decay. I was affirmed that as I made these bold declarations, there was high enthusiasm and positive acclamation with loud shouts of "Amen! Amen!" from the congregation.
- I emphasised that we were not going out to condemn them, but rather to understand why they were given to this lifestyle, knowing the dangers of HIV/AIDS and other sexually transmitted infections. We were going out there to learn and help to create a response to the needs we would have discovered.

From these discussions we learnt a lot:

1. Due to a combined impact of AIDS-related deaths of key family providers/heads, and the destabilisation of households caused by escalating poverty levels, many young girls ended up attempting to earn money by marketing their bodies for sex. As such they had become an extremely high-risk group in regard to the dangers posed by growing HIV/AIDS infections.

2. It was most shocking to discover that some ladies interviewed during our night outreach visits claimed they were married and were on the streets with the full 'consent' of their respective husbands, as this was their chosen way of ensuring livelihood at home. However, the ladies in question also complained that at times they did not benefit from the money earned, as it would be surrendered to their husbands who were in the habit of squandering the money on alcohol.
3. It was also shocking to discover that some of the girls on the streets were as young as 13 years of age. The oldest met were in the mid-30s range. Some of the girls were actually making money on behalf of entire families.
4. Asked whether they would be willing to consider other means of survival, all the girls interviewed responded in the affirmative, that they were ready to take any such alternative, as they were aware the risk borne by their continuation in prostitution. This was a window of opportunity we swiftly seized.

This set the stage for the intervention called 'Operation Paseli'. *Paseli* is the name of the street along which our church is located, which was/is frequented by numerous commercial sex workers.

Following many weeks of interaction with the target group, some girls were prepared to enrol into a Skills Training course that had been designed for other vulnerable women at the church. The first few were offered temporary shelter to facilitate easier access to counselling services.

An integrated group of 30 widows, including a few rehabilitated former sex workers, completed the first phase and were granted micro-credit loans and sewing machines to assist them towards income generation. Some testified that, for the first time in their lives, they were now involved in honest and gainful activity.

The programme progressed into a second phase of skills training with an enrolment of 50 commercial sex workers who underwent gradual rehabilitation. Those enrolled soon began to show strong commitment to a changed lifestyle and became very consistent in attending training sessions, twice a week. A third of those in training were actually recruited by peers who simply asked if they could bring their friends from the streets.

Skills courses taught included:
- Life skills and values of chastity, fidelity and fulfilled living
- Personal hygiene
- Basic home economics and nutrition
- Basic tailoring and design
- Making tie and dye materials
- How to start a small business
- Budgeting and managing of finances
- HIV/AIDS and the dangers of high risk sexual lifestyles.

The courses, which were covered over a six-month duration, also included individual psychosocial counselling, as well as interactive activities to enhance interpersonal skills. Exposure visits to hospitals, hospices, etc. become an important way for initiating discussions on HIV/AIDS and personal responsibility. Other exposure visits linked directly to some of the skills taught. For instance, a clothing factory was visited to interface with the tailoring course.

Since the inception of Operation Paseli, there has been a clear reduction in the number of young girls on Paseli road at night. A number of those rehabilitated have assumed social stability in society and are now agents of change. Three colourful graduation ceremonies eventually followed the successive completion of training programmes (graduating 30, 70, and 90 respectively). After that another class of 100 was enrolled.

THE CIRCLE OF HOPE (COH): PROVIDING FREE ANTI-RETROVIRAL TREATMENT (ART) AND COMMUNITY OUTREACH TO THOUSANDS OF PERSONS LIVING POSITIVELY WITH HIV/AIDS

The COH initiative was founded in 2003 following 8 years of our growing personal pastoral involvement with church members who voluntarily disclosed their HIV+ status to my wife and I expressing the need for care. These individuals also expressed a deep longing for interaction with other persons of a similar status.

We sought the permission of these individuals concerned to allow us make an announcement in church, for those interested in meeting others with the intent of forming a support group. The call was for the group to meet on a particular weekend, at our home. Sixteen ladies and one gentleman turned up! So, right there, in the backyard of our home, the support group that later chose its name as Circle of Hope was born!

In November 2003 it was formalised into a congregation-based support group for persons living positively with HIV. The number eventually grew from 17 to nearly 100 people, as brethren met regularly to devise strategies to compliment care, treatment and support ideals. There were also discussion on prevention of HIV/AIDS through the promotion of sexual abstinence and marital fidelity, maintaining the congregation as a support base.

In September 2005, the COH Family Care Centre Clinic was established, to address growing needs for HIV/AIDS treatment and care, including the specific provision of Voluntary Counselling and Testing (VCT) and Anti-Retroviral Therapy (ART). The initiative was officially launched on 18 January 2004 by the Vice President of the Republic of Zambia.

To date, COH has counselled and tested over 7,429 people, of whom 5,326 are HIV+ and have been enrolled on care. Of the number that are positive, 2,310 are currently on full ART, of which 516 are children. A group in excess of 200 community adherence personnel, care givers and counsellors have sensitised, educated and monitored clients on treatment in their homes. Approximately 80 people visit the COH Centre per day, while 120 patients are enrolled monthly.

Enrolment entails that one undergoes voluntary pre-test and post-test counselling, and for people who are found HIV+ immediate treatment is commenced, with one month's supply of medication. From then on they return to the centre once a month, for review and medication. Before their return to the entre, they are visited individually at home.

The visits ensure effective adherence to treatment for those on ART as well as to check on those on care but not yet on treatment. This is to monitor their health and remind them of their review or appointment dates. The patients are also given information on their nutritional as well as psycho-social needs. To this end, nutritional supplement packs have been distributed and income-generating skills have been taught and developed, particularly for under privileged and disadvantaged clients. Evidently, the home visits are the strength of the COH intervention.

BEHAVIOUR CHANGE COMMUNICATION

Noting the importance of lifestyle in the prevention of new HIV infections, COH has championed and utilised behaviour change communication through various media including radio, television and billboards.

This outreach campaign has advised the youth and adults to live responsible lifestyles of abstinence, positive living, and faithfulness to one sexual partner within marriage. These programs have contributed greatly to the reduction of stigma and discrimination by encouraging open discussions about HIV/AIDS and sexuality in a society that is largely conservative and traditional.

It is worth noting that COH does not engage in condom distribution. However, its Outreach Team provides general public health information for allowable usage of condoms for discordant married couples (where one is HIV+ while the spouse may be negative) and cases where both husband and wife are HIV+. This minimises re-infection that would otherwise lead to increased viral load.

Plans are currently underway to source funding to erect a hospital on a demarcated piece of land the church has apportioned to COH at the Lazarus Project. The intended facility will be at a district hospital level in Zambia (25-50 beds), to include both general out-patient and in-patient medical services, while sustaining current free ART.

POLITICAL BATTLES OVER HUMAN RIGHTS AT HIGH LEVEL

The deep level of engagement in the AIDS fight has brought us face-to-face with policy challenges at high levels, both locally and globally.

From December 2007 until August 2010, I served as Chairperson of the General Constitutional Principles Committee of a 500 member statutory National Constitutional Conference (NCC), mandated by the then Zambian Parliament, to examine, debate and adopt public proposals to alter the Zambian constitution.

As Chairman of this Committee of the NCC, I presided over committee sittings convened to cover specific terms of reference as mandated by the NCC, to examine and recommend the adoption of underlying constitutional principles to be enshrined in the normative section of the new Zambian constitution and upon which the rest of the substantive constitution was to be based. The committee consisted of 44 persons, including 8 MPs and the then Vice President of the Republic of Zambia.

One of the most demanding sections of the draft constitution had to deal with economic, social and cultural rights in the constitution and the Bill of Rights. In particular, the human rights issues focused around issues of sexuality.

In the public arena, outside the NCC, general debate calling for inclusion of the said rights in the Bill of Rights raged on. This was largely led by donor-aided civil society organisations, some of whom it was feared were projecting their funders' agenda. This was more so in response to the fact that the NCC draft had strengthened the marriage clause by specifying that marriage in Zambia should be between two adults (minimum age of 18) of the opposite sex. The draft specified, further, that same sex marriages would stand prohibited.

Although there were no specific public statements locally opposing this direction, the ensuing policies from many donor countries represented in Zambia indicated under-currents that are likely to gain intensity in terms of pressure surrounding human rights issues. This kind of pressure is likely to go on for a long time in Africa for as long as the budgets of African states are hugely reliant on donor aid.

For instance, in the wake of global resources that are channelled into Africa to fight HIV/AIDS, there is now a general call from donor countries for African states to adopt a rights-based approach in HIV interventions along with an expectation that these rights are tied to donor aid.

Some recent public statements illustrate how high on the global priority list the Lesbian, Gay, Bisexual, Transgender and Intersex (LGBTI) agenda has ascended. Three high level statements deserve mention:
1. The call by Prime Minister Cameron at a Commonwealth gathering in Australia, to tie donor aid to the acceptance of LGBT rights (30th October, 2011).
2. A similar call from the then USA Secretary of State Hilary Clinton (Geneva, 6th December, 2011).
3. A statement by UN Secretary General Ban Ki Moon at the African Union Summit in Addis Ababa in January 2012, calling for recognition of sexual orientation as a rights issue.

4. A statement by UN Secretary General Ban Ki Moon to the Zambian Parliament (24th February, 2012) made him the first UN official to ever mention sexual orientation as a matter of human rights on site, to Zambian legislators.

While there may be visible injustices that the church should address whenever need arises, it is clear that it's the highly emotive issues of the so-called alternative sexual lifestyles that are more likely to continue topping the advocacy agenda in many African States. The church must therefore brace itself to engage the society as credibly as possible. Other human rights related topics likely to gain momentum include abortion rights and what is now termed 'comprehensive sexuality education for young people'.

Another instance was witnessed at one Special Session of the United Nations General Assembly that I was privileged to attend in New York. I was amazed at the evident vigour with which the matter of HIV and human rights was debated.

The June 2011 Session was focused on universal access to treatment for HIV. Nearly each and every western state that made their statement to the General Assembly, included some sort of call for other member States to recognise the rights of LGBTIs, injection drug users and sex workers, along with open demands that States where such practices are legally prohibited should decriminalise them.

Negotiating a consensus document as a final outcome of this 65th Session of the UN General Assembly became very challenging. Point 29 read:

> *Note that many national HIV prevention strategies inadequately focus on populations that epidemiological evidence shows are at higher risk, specifically men who have sex with men, people who inject drugs and sex workers, and further note, however, that each country should define the specific populations that are key to its epidemic and response, based on the epidemiological and national context.*

What was most disconcerting was that when the Islamic Republics of Iran and of Syria raised objections to Point 29 on the basis of well articulated social, moral and religious grounds, some UN members booed the distinguished representatives of these States. On the other hand, when Brazil and Mexico spoke in support of the furtherance of efforts to promote LGBTI rights, a significant number of delegates spontaneously applauded. A statement from a representative of the Holy See called for a preference of abstinence over condom promotion in prevention strategies. Again a section of the House booed loudly.

AN ONGOING BATTLE

Clearly, significant biases still abide, despite the growing body of evidence that behaviour change is central to winning the fight against HIV. The danger with labels and stereotypes is that they tend to belittle some of the available epidemiological evidence and instead perpetrate a subtle institutionalised stigma against particular, traditional but now seemingly unconventional programmatic strategies, such as the ones the church propagates.

While the aforementioned narrative highlights daunting challenges faced in the fight against AIDS, all is not lost! The good news is that the HIV incidence has begun to drop in many countries. Thus the budget for taking care of people on treatment will stop going up.

The other good news is that we are still the *church* of Jesus Christ. It is my contention that the church has thus far not fully employed its spiritual resources of dedicated prayer for the needed AIDS resources.

There is a need to reposition HIV/AIDS within the core business of the church in which we must now view AIDS missiologically as the newest door to mission; the essence of *Missio Dei* (the mission of God). In this respect, it is an opportune entry point for reaching deep inside the hearts of those infected and affected. What Africa is battling with in the face of the AIDS pandemic is a notion which we could term lightly as a seeming "covenant with death" (Isa. 28:15) – obviously at serious variance with the essence of our gospel message. The gospel message is about life and hope, now and hereafter! Thus it is a "day of good news" (2 Kings 7:3-11). Our spiritual resources are mightier than the 'strongholds' posed by HIV/AIDS (2 Cor. 10:3-5).

I propose that we embark on specific prayer actions to God to open new doors for opportunities and financial resources towards this 'new' mission frontier. The church has had a reasonable level of such resources for spreading the gospel in general. Why not still believe God who is the one expanding our mission frontier for adequate provision for the same? I challenge us to think and pray outside the traditional box!

A PERSONAL NOTE

My own journey and experience with AIDS reached a seminal level of personal application of transformation in 1992 when my brother-in-law, Charles, was diagnosed HIV+ in the late stages of a debilitating ailment that had him bedridden for many months.

On a particular Thursday morning, I sensed the leading of the Holy Spirit to share the gospel with him and he readily accepted Jesus as his personal Saviour. Later that day, he was discharged from the hospital for home care. Barely three days later, he passed on to glory, right at his home. His wife had died two years earlier, leaving a young boy of five years, as their only surviving offspring.

Those who were by the bed-side just before Charles died say that he suddenly begun to speak (after having mysteriously lost his voice the previous day) and requested the family members to sing two hymns – 'It's not an easy road' and 'It is well with my soul', soon after which he broke spontaneously into a language the persons there could not understand. Clearly he appeared to be deeply engaged in some intense form of prayer and he looked really happy. Following that, Charles lifted his hand, said bye and died! Such an enduring expression of hope and faith in the face of pain can only come from a whole gospel shared with persons who eventually find their wholeness in Jesus Christ, the Lord over death.

NETWORKING LOCAL CHURCHES, FOR HIV/AIDS INTERVENTIONS
FRANCIS MKANDAWIRE

Francis Mkandawire is General Secretary, EAM (Evangelical Association of Malawi), Malawi.

Integral mission involves bringing about the 'shalom' of God to communities who are experiencing hardships and intense suffering, including those suffering the HIV/AIDS pandemic.

Micah Network, following Lausanne, says that, "Integral mission or holistic transformation, is the proclamation and declaration of the gospel. It is not simply that evangelism and social involvement are being done alongside each other. Rather, in integral mission, our proclamation has social consequences as we call people to love and repentance in all areas of life. And our social involvement work will have the evangelistic consequences as we bear witness to the transformation grace of Jesus Christ." This is the main calling of the church.

HIV/AIDS SITUATIONS IN MALAWI

The first HIV/AIDS case in Malawi was diagnosed in 1985. HIV is more prevalent among urban residents than rural. The national prevalence rate among those aged 15-49 years old is now at 11% (2009) down from 14.4% in 2003. There are nearly 100,000 new HIV infections in Malawi annually, with at least half of these occurring among young people aged 15-24 and nearly the same number of deaths. As of 2009, there was an estimated 920,000 people, including children, who were living with HIV and AIDS.

The number of orphans has increased significantly with current estimates being at well over one million, nearly half of whom are due to HIV and AIDS and related factors. In total there were 1,278,000 Orphans and Vulnerable Children (OVC) in Malawi in 2006. The number of OVC has overwhelmed the extended family system and this has led to the emergence of child-headed households. Many orphans, especially girls, face the challenge of accessing food. In addition, households cannot afford school fees and other related costs, hence the children drop out of school.

The impacts of the epidemic started being felt in the early 1990s, and affected individuals, households, communities and the nation. The impact on health has been most evident, with AIDS mortality increasing from 22,000 in 1985 to 87,000 in 2005. AIDS has reduced life expectancy from an estimated 56 years to 36 years at present. Owing to the epidemic, tuberculosis has increased from about 5,000 cases in 1985 to about 30,000 cases now. Nearly 80% of the people with pulmonary tuberculosis are also HIV+. HIV/AIDS also increased demands on Malawi's healthcare system: more than 50% of the hospital beds in Malawi are occupied by people suffering from AIDS-related illnesses. The epidemic has increased the workload of the already poorly staffed Ministry of Health, and households are spending a good proportion of their resources to care for chronically ill persons.

The HIV/AIDS epidemic has a profound impact on Malawi's human capacity, as it mostly affects economically productive people. Between 1990 and 2006 the Ministries of Education (MoE), Agriculture (MoAFS) and Health (MoH), as well as the Malawi Police Service lost 1,550 teachers, 5,533 workers, and 2,552 police officers respectively, and the major cause of attrition was death. Most of the staff who died were aged less than 40 years, indicating AIDS mortality. AIDS deaths prevent the civil service effectively delivering public services like health and education. The same situation exists in private companies where many skilled personnel have died from AIDS, and productivity has gone down because of absenteeism and death of productive members. Government and employers face high costs to take care of the sick, pay life insurance claims, death gratuities and the cost of burials.

The epidemic contributes to food insecurity at household level as over 80% of Malawians depend on agriculture for food and a source of income. During illness, agricultural work is neglected or abandoned, negatively affecting agricultural output. The loss of adult labour leads families to leave the land to fallow. Orphans may not have acquired enough skills to perform some agricultural activities; hence they may resort to simpler activities such as petty trading, transactional sex and prostitution. Reduction in human resources also negatively affects the ability of agricultural institutions to provide agricultural support services. It has been estimated that by 2020 Malawi's agricultural workforce will be 14% smaller than it would have been without HIV and AIDS.

It is important that the HIV and AIDS epidemic is contained so that these impacts are reversed.

THE CHURCH'S RESPONSE TO THE EPIDEMIC

The church is a very influential institution in Africa. In Europe Governments have taken responsibility to cater for the basic needs of its people; not so in Africa. In the case of Malawi, close to 63% of the educational institutions are provided by the church operating under Association of Educators in Malawi (ACEM). In health, 43% of the health institutions are owned by churches through Christian Health Association of Malawi (CHAM). There is no other institution so strategically positioned to tackle the HIV/AIDS pandemic the way the church can. The church has these distinctive strengths:

(i) Compassionate ministry

Church involvement in mitigating HIV/AIDS impact is a mandate given to the church from God. "True religion that pleases God is to take care on orphans and widows in their hour of need" (James 1:27).

(ii) Grassroots structure

In most of the countries, especially in Southern Africa where the pandemic is highest, the church has permanent structures present at grassroots level in most of the communities, unlike other NGOs or even the Government.

(iii) Holistic approach

HIV/AIDS is not only a health issue, but also has an economic, social and spiritual dimension. Only the church can tackle, holistically and effectively, the problem from all these fronts. No other institution has such an advantageous position.

(iv) Behaviour change message

It is generally agreed that 'Behaviour Change' is probably the only sure solution to addressing the HIV/AIDS crisis. The church, being a strong advocate for high moral principles, is the best vehicle to effectively address this. The role of churches in mitigating the spread and impact of the

HIV/AIDS pandemic is therefore very crucial. It is encouraging to note that many secular bodies, including governments, especially in Southern Africa, are beginning to understand and appreciate this unique role which only the church can play in the fight against HIV/AIDS. The church is now being consulted on social development and other policy formulation forums by both the public and private sector. The church is becoming a key stakeholder in the battle front.

The church in Malawi 'welcomed' the HIV/AIDS epidemic with a mixed reaction. HIV/AIDS was immediately labelled a disease for the immoral. The push for condoms by other activists, as the most effective tool to avoid contracting the disease, only compounded the church's resentment. HIV/AIDS was seen at separate from the life of the church. However, twenty years later, HIV/AIDS has come into our homes, even our own bedrooms. Indeed the church has AIDS. Almost every household has been affected either directly or indirectly.

In 2003, the first ecumenical conference on HIV/AIDS was organised by the three Christian mother bodies, namely the Evangelical Association of Malawi, Malawi Council of Churches and the Episcopal Conference of Malawi. The theme of the Conference was breaking the silence on HIV/AIDS. There had been a sense of denial that the church had HIV/AIDS and needed to get involved in the fight.

During the conference, a survey was conducted to determine the levels of stigma and discrimination against people living with HIV and AIDS. A question was put over to them: "Would they allow an HIV/AIDS Christian to take leadership role in the church?" Over 60% of the respondents categorically said, "No!" About 30% said they would decide if/when the situation arose. The rest did not know what they would do. The conference programme included testimonies from some PLWAs (People Living With HIV/AIDS). The church was moved to learn that even some of the well respected church leaders in their midst were HIV+. For many, it was their first time to hear first hand experiences of those who are positive.

This conference agreed to break the silence on HIV/AIDS by the church. Church leaders were challenged to face reality and accept that HIV/AIDS was with us and we needed to learn to live with it.

During the conference several gaps were identified in the church's response. Firstly, it was noted that though some churches were responding, the initiatives were uncoordinated and lacked resources. This later led to the establishment of the Malawi Interfaith AIDS Association (MIAA) by the three Christian bodies to spearhead the coordination of the faith response. Muslims were later included to give the institution its interfaith nature.

The second gap that was identified was the lack of qualified counsellors in the churches. The HIV/AIDS pandemic has brought about great demand for psycho-social counselling services. Consequently, a year later the Ecumenical Counselling Centre was established, by the same Christian mother bodies, with the aim of developing the capacity of churches in counselling.

THE EVANGELICAL ASSOCIATION OF MALAWI (EAM)'S RESPONSE

EAM is an umbrella body for 58 church denominations and 50 Christian organisations united to proclaim the gospel of our Lord Jesus Christ through word and deeds, through the local churches.

In the few years EAM has been implementing the HIV/AIDS Programme, a new concept of working through the local churches in a community has been piloted. This is called the HIV/AIDS Local Churches Consortium approach.

Goal and programme location

The goal of the programme is to contribute to the reduction of new HIV and sexually transmitted infections, to alleviate the suffering of HIV/AIDS infected and affected people, and to mitigate the impact of the epidemic. The programme is now being implemented in 16 out of the 28 districts in the country. A total of 630 churches are involved in the programme, representing a population approximately 112,000 people. It is the intention of the EAM to saturate the whole country with local church Consortiums as part of its implementation of integral missions through the local church.

How the local HIV/AIDS consortiums work

The HIV/AIDS Churches Consortiums comprise of different denominations in a particular geographical location of not more than 20 km radius. The churches are assisted to design, manage and implement together one huge HIV/AIDS programme with several interventions. The programme is popularly known as the 'One Enemy, One Body, One

Programme' concept. The targeted locations are divided into smaller manageable areas commonly known as Consortium Zones to serve as programme activity implementation areas.

In set up, all the church leaders of the congregations participating in the Consortium form the General Assembly, which is the policy making body of the programme. The General Assembly then establishes two other structures; the Zone Committees, made up of leaders within the zone, and an Executive Committee for the Consortium comprising of selected ten leaders amongst the church leadership. The leadership of the Consortium is encouraged to take on board other additional technical people from various fields like health, agriculture, social welfare, chiefs and businessmen within the catchment are of the community.

The Executive Committee, in turn, establishes a Consortium Programme Office and recruits a Consortium Programme Coordinator and an assistant. These become responsible for the coordination role within the Consortium and with other agencies outside the Consortium, including EAM offices at regional level.

The General Assembly also identifies men, women, boys and girls from various congregations to be trained as service providers, working as volunteers in the selected thematic areas of interventions. Currently the five priority areas are:

- Adult and youth peer education;
- Home based care:
- Community based child care for orphans and vulnerable children;
- People Living with HIV/AIDS support (PLWA); and
- Pastors and church leaders.

Lately, some Consortiums have started to target traditional chiefs and community leaders as well. These are important stakeholders in developmental decision-making processes in the villages, besides being the custodians on culture.

At each level, i.e. the General Assembly, the Executive Committee, the coordinating office and service providers, the EAM regional offices provides:

- Thorough training;
- Technical support;
- Mentoring and networking.

Each programme area has a man and a woman developed as trainers and supervisors, who in turn train others and provide the necessary supervision.

Role of EAM in the programme

The Evangelical Association of Malawi HIV/AIDS Regional offices have the responsibility to build the capacity of the churches and church organisations to ensure effective and efficient, professional and coherent programming, management, implementation and service delivery of the programme activities. The programme seeks to mobilise and equip, systematically and effectively, all key groups in the targeted communities to mitigate the impact of the HIV/AIDS crisis.

Basic training is provided to:
- Volunteers from local churches in home based care;
- Community based child care centre volunteers;
- Peer educators for youth and life skills training.

As regards the general management of the Consortium, the Coordinator and the main committee are trained in project management and implementation, financial management, reporting, proposal writing and general fund raising.

Recently, other specialised trainings addressing specific concerns have also been incorporated. These include gender, economic justice issues, paralegal services to victims of injustices and stigmatisation, and small scale business management courses. Those who have done well in such courses, especially the PLWAs, have been introduced to loan facilities offered by banks and other financing institutions. In most of the cases, the training is provided by experts from either government or the private sector to ensure quality in compliance with Malawi Government requirements.

The Programme distinguishes the following groups as the priority rights holders of the programme:

People living with HIV infection and AIDS

PLWAs are encouraged to establish support groups in their respective zones. In addition to suffering from HIV/AIDS-related infections and diseases, people living with the virus face a tremendous obstacle of survival in life as a result of stigma and discrimination that creates loneliness and depression.

This group which accommodates those with chronic illnesses is a priority group of rights holders in the Programme. EAM's role to this group has been:
- Training of home based care givers – 20 per zone (ten men and ten women).
- Provision of bicycles to HBC volunteers, since most of them travel long distances.
- Provision of bicycle ambulances to assist those completely incapacitated and unable to travel to access treatment. So far EAM has provided one ambulance per zone. There are normally five zones per consortium.
- Ensure that the PLWAs are food secure. Where necessary, connect them with agencies which can help them with agricultural inputs or start-up loans for small business.
- Provide paralegal training to consortiums in order that they may fight for the rights of PLWAs and the disadvantaged groups in the community.
- Provision of fertilisers and agricultural inputs to the chronically ill, resources permitting.

The youth (boys and girls)

The silent voices of boys and girls in decision making, and the recipient role they are positioned in by the community has made them become more vulnerable than adults – especially girls. EAM primarily focuses on capacity building of this group, mainly focusing on the following:
- Peer educators training of trainers (20 youths trained per zone);
- Life-skills for the youths, in fields such as carpentry, tailoring, agricultural skills and small scale business development;
- Drama and sports outreach programs;
- Facilitating girls and the most vulnerable youth to remain in school by provision of basic needs such as fees and note books – their local churches are now taking over the responsibility.

Orphans and vulnerable children
Children from poor families, single or child-headed families, parent(s) with disabilities and abuse families suffering child abuse are equally vulnerable. These too are a priority group of rights holders for the programme.
Activities for the group include the following:
- Two weeks training of CBCC care givers. The training is provided by experts from the Ministry of Children and Social welfare. Four people per a zone (two men and two women).
- Establishment of the CBCC centres in each zone.
- Feeding programme for the vulnerable children in the CBCC in each zone. The churches through the Consortium contribute the food and take turns to cook for the children.

Chiefs and traditional leaders
These are involved in HIV/AIDS Awareness workshops which focus on:
- Gender and human rights issues;
- Cultural issues which promote the spread of HIV/AIDS;
- Good governance sensitisation;
- Economic justice issues.

Pastors and key church leaders
Similarly their workshops concentrate on:
- Evangelism and discipleship training;
- Advocacy and good governance;
- HIV/AIDS awareness, prevention, care and support.

ADDITIONAL INTERVENTIONS
EAM, with support from Tearfund and Irish Aid, has introduced new interventions to local churches consortium programmes. EAM is implementing a three-year HIV programme focusing on Improving Parent and Child Outcomes (IMPACT). The project is using a comprehensive approach to Prevent Parent to Child Transmission (PPTCT) of HIV. Currently the programme is being piloted. The overall aim of the project is to contribute to a reduction of HIV prevalence, and maternal and child mortality. The main objective is to reduce vertical transmission of HIV to less than 7% by 2014.

Churches working together with other stakeholders and government

Churches have been mobilised fully and are working together with traditional leaders, community and government to help reduce maternal and child mortality and promote male involvement in PPTCT activities in the two communities.

Introduction of 'mother buddy' concept

This has been seen to be powerful as a strategy that has increased the number of pregnant women from communities with access to an Anti-Natal Clinic (ANC). 'Mother buddies' are mothers living HIV+ who have managed to give birth to children who are negative, due to adherence to instructions as given by the medical practitioners. This has also increased uptake and access of health services which will significantly help to reduce maternal and child mortality in the two communities.

Partnership with government on IMPACT project

Through the IMPACT project, we have seen churches and government partnerships growing strong in working towards reducing maternal and child mortality through provision of staff, transport and testing kits during church HIV Testing and Counselling (HTC) mobile campaigns in the two communities. This partnership has also been seen through meetings with Ministry of Health staff at district and health centre level, and Disaster Emergencies Committee (DEC) and Domestic Abuse Counselling Clinic (DACC) meetings

Male involvement in PMTC

Men have traditionally been reluctant to get involved with HIV/AIDS awareness activities. A nurse at Namadzi Health centre, Mrs Banda, said, "We have seen an increase in male partners and their pregnant women coming to ANC for services. Initially in October to December, 2011, in a week the attendance was three to four pregnant couples, but now as of October 2012 we are able to register 15 to 16 partners of pregnant women in a week. This gives us a signal that the attitudes of men have started to change as a result of interventions implemented in IMPACT project like PPTCT, mother buddies and other interventions'."

Lessons Learnt

Ownership of the program
There is strength in joint ownership of the programme by the churches and the community as a whole, instead of a single church or organisation.

Duplication of services significantly reduced
This has also reduced the duplication of services and unnecessary competition amongst the churches in the targeted community, as the Church Consortium management and service delivery teams look at community needs collectively. Further, since the Consortium approach generally focuses on the needs of people in an area other than church affiliation, resources are thus maximised.

Unity amongst participating churches strengthened
The programme has promoted unity amongst the churches in the community. The church and not denomination is seen working in the communities, attracting more and more demands for services. Bringing different denominations together in managing and implementing one programme is, from a spiritual perspective, a miracle on its own! This emphasises the focal point being the suffering community and not church membership.

United church voice
It has enabled the churches and community leaders to speak with one voice on specific issues of concern to their respective areas. This includes lobbying for a greater share of resources and technical support from the District Assemblies. Some local Church Consortium groups have already managed to link up with their respective District Assemblies for support. Others have managed to attract support from other donor agencies both locally and internationally. Doctrinal differences are proving not to be a barrier. The approach has demonstrated the highest possibility of leaders of different denominations joining hands when it comes to wanting to address a crisis and, in this case, an epidemic.

Wider coverage of information and messages
More people can be reached in a short period of time than would have been the case using a single church structure. In this approach, within a short time, information can easily be passed to a huge population in the targeted zones.

Stigma and discrimination
Stigma is collectively being dealt with. The consortiums have registered a growing number of PLWHAs seeking services from the local participating churches and individual Christians feel much freer than before.

Transparency and accountability
Unfaithfulness and dishonesty in programme management, implementation and service delivery is minimised, as there are numerous eyes and ears watching and listening. There are adequate structures to provide the much needed checks and balances.

Capacity building
Training is made easy and cheaper since it is the church in the community which is targeted, instead of individual congregations.

Establishment of networks and linkages with other service providers
Consortiums are encouraged to link with other existing services providers within the community such as NGOs or relevant government agencies. So far strategic alliances have been established with other service providers such as VCT providers, hospitals or clinics for treatment and ARVs, agencies supporting PLWAs, counselling agencies for psycho-social support, Social Welfare offices at district level responsible for child development, etc. The actual cost of running a Consortium is therefore spread over a number of stakeholders.

Integrated approach to HIV/AIDS
HIV/AIDS is multi-faceted. The programme has to be open and flexible to other interventions as need arises. For instances lately, nutrition, IGAs and small business enterprises for PLWAs and orphans have been incorporated. In other Consortiums, a strong component of advocacy has been brought in,

working closely with traditional leaders to revisit some harmful cultural practices. We are now considering including a component of water and sanitation in all the child development interventions in most of the Consortiums.

Cross learning and sharing of experiences

Regular forums for learning and refresher sessions have been organised for service providers or management teams drawn from various Consortiums. Orientation visits between Consortiums are also being done. In the case of youths, drama competition and soccer tournaments are taking place between the various Consortiums. Cross-learning and sharing of experiences is greatly enhanced through the Consortium approach.

EMERGING ISSUES

Global economic down-turns

The general global economic disturbances has had an impact on the church's response to the crisis in the short and long term. In particular, food prices in Malawi have risen up by over 60% over the past two years,. This is greatly affecting the ability of PLWAs on Anti-Retroviral Therapy (ART) to access appropriate food. Transport prices have also gone up by a similar margin due to fuel increases. Most of the ART patients in rural areas are experiencing problems traveling to district centres every month to access drugs. Another major concern at the moment is the ability of PLWAs accessing agricultural inputs such as fertilisers and seeds for their nutritional requirements. Prices have gone up by 400% over a period of one year due to global foreign exchange disturbances.

How integral is our integral mission?

The ministry of our Lord Jesus Christ was holistic, addressing the whole needs of the human being – spiritually, socially and physically. However, experience has proved that much effort has to be made to make interventions really integral. The need to establish clear holistic indicators in the programs is critical to ensure that important pillars to our integral mission's interventions are not overlooked. Some evangelical donors are specifically including in their project design spiritual indicators to show spiritual transformation.

Research and documentation

There is inadequate research and documentation taking place of the work of churches in area of HIV/AIDS. The only available work is by secular organisations and institutions often not taking into account the fundamental values which churches hold on to very highly. For instance, in Malawi the secular NGOs pushing for wholesale condom distribution in schools, including primary schools, have been claiming that this action is necessary as the majority of the children in schools are not abstaining from sex. From the reports we are getting from our workers in these schools and colleges, the majority of the children do abstain and they need to be encouraged accordingly. In the absence of any research to strengthen such a proposition, the church seems to have no grounds to influence key decision makers.

Investment in capacity building

For churches to be empowered to take up the challenge of integral mission in their communities, through the local Churches Consortium Program, there is need for a substantial investment in capacity building/community training and empowerment in programme management and service delivery as regards HIV/AIDS interventions. Sustainability of the programme is closely linked to the levels of investment, whether in terms of resources or time. Most of the local churches consortiums where EAM phased out funding are still operational on their own without any support from EAM. This is so because of the massive investment which had been made in training and development of skills and knowledge and change of attitudes in the members of the churches and community at large.

CONCLUSION

Integral mission is a must for the churches, more so now in the face of this crisis before us. If all other stakeholders fail to tackle the HIV/AIDS pandemic, it will be unfortunate. However, the church in integral mission, addressing the pandemic, holding out the gospel of Jesus Christ through word and deeds, is capable of ensuring that God's people are living dignified lives on earth, even in the face of trials and sufferings. This is the abundant life Jesus Christ promised in John 10:10. It is therefore imperative for evangelicals, worldwide, to come out from our comfort zones and begin to make a difference in our communities as we, as his church, serve his people for Jesus Christ.

Satisfying the Thirsty, by Water and Sanitation Projects

Kenneth Twinamatsiko

Kenneth Twinamatsiko is Communications and Advocacy officer, Diocese of Kigezi Water and Sanitation Project, Uganda.

Uganda is a beautiful, landlocked country in East Africa, roughly the size of the UK. Winston Churchill called it the 'pearl of Africa'. With a population around 34 million, the majority live in rural areas. It has a varied terrain, mountainous with many lakes in the south and west, and though there is plenty of water in the rainy season, it does not always come at the right time, in steady amounts, or in appropriate places.

Although there is a considerable annual rainfall in the Kigezi area there is also a lack of access to safe water to ensure sustainable Water and Sanitation (WATSAN) services, good hygiene, and development initiatives for improved livelihoods. These problems are worsened by a lack of human and material capacity to address them. With a combination of distant and unreliable water sources and poor hygiene practices, water is contaminated by human and animal excreta. Water sources are found in the valley bottoms while people reside on hill tops reserving low fertile soils for agriculture. Typically people need to drop down more than 200m on steep slopes to reach the water, and another, more arduous, 200m to take it back to the houses at the top. It is not uncommon for girls and women (rarely men!) to have to walk three or four hours daily to fetch the water. Natural water resources are under pressure from competing uses (e.g. individual local farmers diverting the streams into their own land) and most of them become depleted, leaving stagnant pools of water which puts life at danger.

Kigezi Diocese Water and Sanitation Programme (KDWSP)

KDWSP is a faith based organisation aimed at meeting the needs of the rural poor and water stressed communities in Diocese of Kigezi, in SW Uganda. Since its inception in 1986, KDWSP has evolved and grown from grace to grace in providing safe clean water to rural communities of Kigezi.

It was started by the late Bishop Kivengyere with an aim of providing safe water to girls of Bishop Kivengyere Girls' School which was established on the top of a hill, necessitating girls to go for a round trip of five kilometres to fetch water from the steams below. Tearfund UK has been supporting it in partnership since its inception.

KDWSP now has a formidable reputation for providing clean water to about one eighth of Uganda. It has been judged one of the best NGOs in WATSAN service delivery and has twice won the National Best Performing NGO Award from the Ministry of Water and Environment. When in full operation, KDWSP employs over 45 staff members with an average budget of $850,000 serving all people irrespective of social status, religious and political affiliations.

KDWSP PRINCIPLES

Vision
- Healthy and self reliant members of the church and community.

Objectives
- To provide improved and sustainable water and sanitation services in targeted communities in Kabale district.
- To equip the local church, NGOs, CBOs, other dioceses, community members and interested individuals with skills and best practices in WATSAN.
- To mainstream cross-cutting issues of HIV/AIDS, environmental sustainability, family planning and food security.
- To advocate for improved and equitable access to safe water and sanitation services.

Nationally, the key policy objective of the Directorate of Water Resource Management is,

To manage and develop the water resources of Uganda in an integrated and sustainable manner so as to secure and provide water of adequate quantity and quality for all social and economic needs of the present and future generations with full participation of all stakeholders.

KDWSP works with other stakeholders to ensure:
- well managed water resources and vibrant stakeholders;
- well managed catchment areas (reduction in erosion and lakes silting, vegetation cover, active catchment based management structures, policies being effected);
- more vegetative cover (fruit trees, timber trees) around water sources and both up-stream and down-streams
- self-driven and willing people;
- that competing water uses are realigned to ensure equitable and sustainable utilisation of water resources and water sources (protected springs, gravity schemes and rainwater harvesting tanks).

KDWSP has five key core values and guiding principles; accountability, transparency, integrity, Christ-centeredness, and quality assurance. It is not just concerned with delivering clean water and ensuring healthy living, but, as a part of the local body of Christ, the church, to do so in a holistic way. It is illuminating and thrilling to see the KDWPS logo on the workers' T-shirts, the sides of the car, and across the working yard, which boldly states:

Water is life, Jesus is everlasting life.

KDWSP WORKS THROUGH FOUR MAIN SECTIONS

1. Construction and training at a rain water centre (a centre of excellence in WATSAN)

KDWSP continues to provide safe clean water to the rural poor for both human and animal consumption and production. This is achieved through water development initiatives and diverse technologies developed to suit communities and households in valley bottoms and hilltops. This is accomplished through construction of:
- gravity flow schemes,
- protection of springs,
- rain water tanks and rain water jars in different capacities depending on number of expected users.

The finished projects are followed up with the local community to ensure proper operation and provide sustainability and functionality of the facilities. There are 50 completed gravity flow schemes and protected springs with well-trained management structures and community based caretakers.

Follow-up training is being established to provide skills, knowledge, and information on WATSAN, and resource mobilisation for accountability and marketing to local leaders, churches, CBOs, interested individuals and other NGOs. The training provides a multiplier effect in increasing safe and sustainable water supplies, operation and maintenance of WATSAN facilities, and promotion of self supply. The illiterate trained artisans have built high quality rain water tanks and jars, which is a great source of income to them.

This is also a potential research centre to generate knowledge and technologies and devise solutions to development problems in the sector for holistic community transformation. The community development teams and water and sanitation committees are also trained and periodically refreshed.

2. Capacity development

KDWSP equips the local church, NGOs, CBOs, other dioceses, community members, and interested individuals with skills and best practices in managing WATSAN projects. This training employs a self help group ideology where members are trained to critically appreciate their problems and systemically devise solutions to address them. The trained CBOs, NGOs, dioceses, and individuals are monitored and followed up to assess how they are promoting self-supply as a measure to increase rain water facilities in their communities.

3. Health promotion

Water stressed communities make applications to KDWSP for intervention. The applications are accessed and priority given to those more stressed than others. A KDWSP team of experts visits these communities to ascertain the magnitude of the need and the appropriate technology required to meet this need. From this, community mobilisation meetings are held to discuss and decide on issues of health education, definition of roles and responsibilities, formation and training of committees, and preparation of hardware intervention which is the actual delivery of WATSAN facilities.

Sanitation coverage is still below 50% because behavioural change is a slow, gradual process. This section conducts community sensitisation and training meetings in management of WATSAN projects, resources mobilisation, sanitation and hygiene, safe water chains and community participatory approaches to project implementation. It mainstreams environmental sustainability, food security and nutrition, HIV/AIDS, malaria control, and family planning issues in water and sanitation activities.

Climatic changes have caused landslides, floods, unpredictable seasons and longer dry spells, and have resulted in food shortage, soil erosion, drop in water tables, and water related diseases. It helps to increase knowledge of the links between water, excreta and disease. Population explosion and its negative impact on development, perpetuation of the HIV/AIDS pandemic, malaria and other killer diseases, are discussed in the community meetings.

4. Advocacy and publicity

We lobby the Central and District Government and advocate for new policies and/or by-laws, policy reviews and endorsement for implementation at all levels. Policies relating to equity and inclusion in access of WATSAN services, sustainability and functionality of WATSAN facilities, are promoted. Emphasis on sanitation and hygiene, and environmental conservation, are high on our advocacy agenda for the next three years.

The same section is charged with documenting best practices and sharing them locally and internationally. It is charged with hosting and promoting connected churches programs, hosting programme visitors, Transform teams, volunteers and civil service programs. It develops and disseminates periodic publications about KDWSP works and ensures updates to development partners and management about the progress of work.

ANNUAL ACTIVITIES

Typically, the annual interventions are delivered in two ways – hardware and software.

Hardware
- Construct one large gravity flow scheme of over 27km with 40-55 tap stands, or 2 medium gravity schemes with 30-58 tap stands serving 5,000 – 6,500 community members
- 12 institutional tanks of 20,000 litres for schools, churches and health centres
- 130 ferro-cement tanks of 4000 litres for households
- 600 water jars of 420 litres for households
- Protect 12 normal springs for communities
- 500 sand filters
- 500 sanitary platforms
- 500 tippy taps.

Software
- Train at least four women's groups of 25 members each in ferro-cement tank construction
- Train 80 artisans in rainwater harvesting technologies
- Carry out health education in all new communities including schools and other organisations
- Carry out on-going support follow up to communities worked in previously
- Mainstream HIV/AIDS control, environmental sustainability, family planning and food security training. (Currently KDWSP benefits at least 22,780 people per year)
- Carry out capacity development trainings in integrated development
- Working to increase latrine coverage
- Advocate to overcome advocacy issues, document and share best practices
- Host four Transform teams, 15 groups of programme visitors and four volunteers to share experiences and knowledge.

Since KDWSP was started in 1986 it has achieved the following:
- 50 gravity flow schemes
- 990 protected springs
- 162 institutional rain water tanks (20,000 – 50,000 litres)

- 1,479 ferro-cement tanks (4000 litres)
- 425 rain water jars (1500 litres)
- 10,410 rain water jars (420 litres)
- 660 bio-sand filters
- 456 artisans have been trained in different rain water harvesting technologies
- 5,300 sanitary platforms
- 5,300 tippy taps.

All these are in addition to software interventions and trainings in sanitation and hygiene, water safety plans, community led total sanitation, environmental protection, integrated development, management and sustainability, family planning, HIV/AIDS, food security, community led advocacy initiatives, and resources mobilisation – all aimed at holistic transformation of society.

STORIES OF TRANSFORMATION

Mbazibwa Julius lives on top of the hill and he fetches water from Rutengye tap stand. However he has managed to set up three nursery beds near this tap of pinus patura, tobacco and eucalyptus.

During the dry season like this, I no longer suffer going to the source to fetch water to spray my seedlings on the nursery bed. I have been selling the seedlings and the remaining ones I plant them myself and this has increased on my income.

Rushekyera Catholic Church is making bricks with water from their tap. Turyatemba Vereriano the catechist said that they want to use the bricks to set up other commercial houses in the trading centre alongside other two houses which have shops in the trading centre to generate income.

The church will be getting some good money after building another house and then renting it to those who can use it.

They have completed a new permanent church using the water from the tap installed in the church compound.

Tindimwebwa Frugensi (65-year-old), with his wife Prisca (60-year-old), owns a wine processing plant in Nyanja. Their confession is that this project has been strengthened by the safe water which they now access nearby. In his words Frugensi says,

> If there is any one that has greatly benefitted from the KDWSP, it is me. If it was not for this water project our wine project would have been stopped.

Production was limited due to the difficulty in water hauling – the distance of about 2 km was expensive. To date, because water is within easy reach, production has increased. There is a ready market for the wine – locally as well as outside Kabale District. The availability of water has also helped to improve sanitation and hygiene; the equipment used is constantly washed. The proceeds of this project are helping the family to pay for the children's education, and also support the church. Flugence's family is God-fearing. They have financially contributed in the construction of the church which is almost completed.

Businge Auzobia (43-year-old) married to Katema Benon (50-year-old), is epileptic. She fell in the fire due to her epilepsy. Her face and the right hand were affected. She was assisted by Transform to access medication. She was admitted at Rugarama hospital for two weeks. The Switzerland Transform team paid her transport costs and medical bills. She was attended to and her health has greatly improved. She now goes to church and her spiritual life has improved. She used to take alcohol which increased the risk of getting epileptic attacks. In appreciation of the medical service rendered to her, she has contributed sand found in one of her small pieces of land to construct one of the reservoir tanks of 20,000 litre capacity. She remarked,

> The church is compassionate and loving; they have saved my life. How much can I thank God?

She now accesses safe water from a water tap just around 15 metres from her household. Prior to this, she used to fetch from a stream where the water quality testing exercise done recently showed the number of coli forms was too numerous to be counted!

LESSONS LEARNT
KDWSP emphasises beneficiary contributions, in which the beneficiaries provide as much as they can, often up to 40% in way of provision of local

materials (sand, aggregates, hard core, poles), unskilled labour, food and accommodation for the skilled labourers and a financial contribution, depending on their ability. While the ideal situation would be to subsidise as high as possible, a lower subsidy instils a sense of ownership and still causes the beneficiary to work hard towards raising the required contribution

The programme gives special consideration to the poorest of the poor, the highly disabled, those affected and infected with HIV/AIDS and provides the facilities at full cost.

The household contribution is raised by individual savings over time, group cash rounds, sale of produce and livestock and loans schemes. Institutional contributions are raised by collections from intended beneficiaries, well-wishers, local government support and local revenue.

The KDWSP programme approach is demand driven. The church is the entry point and trainings for various groups (children, men, women, youth, community leaders) are arranged and conducted there. Trainers reside in communities in which they are carrying out health education at household level and home visits. This enables them to facilitate the formation and training of WATSAN committees through which the project is implemented and later maintained. Contributions are collected by the WATSAN committees and an acknowledgement of receipts given. The implementation is participatory, in that the communities are involved at every stage – planning allocation of facilities, providing locally available resources and unskilled labour. The committees are trained to be able to develop their own monitoring indicators, collect data and analyse and provide the programme with quarterly reports. Periodic monitoring is carried out by programme staff and specific needs addressed – refreshing committees, caretakers and training of new committees after every two years. The programme also supports the communities where major repairs are required, providing only what is not locally available in the community. Post-construction monitoring is carried out together with government extension.

The programme trains women groups in ferro-cement tank construction, and local artisans are trained in the construction of rainwater jars. Groups of 30 people have also been trained from the neighbouring county of Rwanda, as well as 40 people from Teso and Kumi Dioceses, students from Technical Colleges and CARITAS.

The programme has set up a rain water harvesting centre to meet training needs and fill the knowledge and skills gaps in promotion of low-cost rain water harvesting technologies. The concept of harvesting water is unfamiliar to many, but is at the heart of much of this work. The rain comes, but is often wasted. If a system of guttering is arranged on the roof of a house this can direct the rain water into the fabricated jars – the rain has been 'harvested' to be used at a later date. Each house has their own jar, the community will have a larger ferro-concrete jar to share. The centre will further be a resource centre for excellence in WATSAN best practices and a research centre to contribute to knowledge for researchers and research users.

KDWSP collaborates very closely with other players in the water and sanitation sub-sector including the District Local Government, training of other organisations like CARITAS, and attends all district and national stakeholder forums on budgeting, monitoring, external evaluation and joint sector reviews. Areas of operations are agreed upon to avoid duplication, specialised skills and knowledge identified for easy outsourcing and sharing of work plans for different organisations to be able to work together.

CHALLENGES

With the current effects of climate change, rainwater harvesting is ideal for water stressed communities. Unpredictable heavy rains have led to lake and river silting, landslides, floods, and heavy erosions leaving galleys and bare surfaces. Exhaustive human activities have led to pollution and depletion of integrated water resources and made a negative impact on water quality and quantity. In response KDWSP has embraced a paradigm shift to integrated water resources management to promote sustainable use of water resources and mitigation of climatic changes effects.

Local material such as sand and stones may not be available for the community. The terrain is difficult, hilly and rocky which affects the budget in terms of more galvanised pipes, stronger HDPE pipes, transport of materials to hard to reach points. The poor road network is bumpy and during the rainy days delivery of staff and material to certain areas is impossible.

IMPACT

As a result of KDWSP interventions, the distance to safe water points has been considerably reduced, which has increased water consumption, and reduced time and energy that would otherwise be wasted in water hauling over long distances. Income generating activities have sprung up because of integrated development trainings. Water and sanitation related diseases have been considerably reduced. Children have enough time to concentrate in their academic tasks, performance has improved and attendances in schools and churches have substantially improved.

The great lesson is that community-led initiatives are more sustainable than those where outsiders provide the services. Being participatory in approach, skills and knowledge are transferred to community through community-based groups and existing local leadership structures. Thus the locals can be trained, revitalised and empowered to lead communities in their active roles and responsibilities throughout the life of the project. Utilisation of already existing management structures helps to avoid duplication and 'reinventing the wheel'. Full participation of community members helps communities to move from vulnerable beneficiaries to project stakeholders and this instils a sense of ownership that enhances sustainability.

TRANSFORMING COMMUNITIES, THROUGH EDUCATION
PHILIPPE OUEDRAOGO

Philippe Ouedraogo is Executive Director, AEAD (Association Evangelique d'Appui au Developpement), Burkina Faso, and Vice President of AOG Church of Burkina Faso.

Burkina Faso is a totally landlocked country with 14 million people in West Africa. It borders Mali in the north and west, Niger in the north-east, Ivory Coast and Ghana in the south, and Togo and Benin in the south-east. Burkina Faso has a tropical climate of the Sudano-Sahelean type characterised by a long dry season from October to April and a short rainy season from May to September. Burkina Faso now has 49 urban towns, 309 rural communes and 8,228 villages. Though French is the official language, there are over fifty different spoken languages, of which Mooré is the most common. 55% of the population is under 15 years old. It is this age group that is concerned with compulsory education.

Burkina Faso faces acute problems due to its geographical location. Being landlocked it depends on neighbouring sea ports located more than 1,000 km away for its commercial development. The only railway connection to Abidjan is largely dysfunctional due to privatisation and the political and economic crisis in Ivory Coast in recent years. Burkina Faso went through severe droughts in 1969, 1974, 1981, and 1984 and 2005, with a locust invasion in 2005. Recently, severe rainfalls caused flooding and widespread loss of homes and farming land. The impact of climate change, the poverty of the farming land, an inappropriate technology in agriculture are all disadvantages that slow down efforts of hard working peasants. However, the government and civil societies such as churches, NGOs and individuals are heavily committed to work together to improve the lives of the population.

THE CONTRIBUTION OF CIVIL SOCIETIES TO GIRLS' AND WOMEN'S EDUCATION

Non-Governmental Organisations (NGOs) represent an important part of civil society in Sub-Saharan Africa (SSA). This sector is largely represented by religious organisations who introduced education before governments. The first missionaries created many schools in SSA. They were the first to introduce both non-formal and formal education, and training in professional skills. The first graduates from these missionaries were those who fought for independence and became the first national leaders after the colonial period. Religious organisations such as the churches and NGOs continue to play a major role in the education sector in SSA in both formal and non-formal sectors. They were the first to establish specialised schools and training institutions that catered for the marginalised groups such as the handicapped, orphans, and vulnerable children. Alongside the churches are Christian NGOs that are specializing in women's and girls' education. Their contributions are highly significant in Burkina Faso.

Illiteracy is still high among the population of Burkina Faso, with an adult literacy currently of 40%. Women are the most affected and each woman aged between 15-49 bears on average 6.2 children. The Burkina Faso Strategy for Growth and Sustainable Development (SCAAD) states that: "Education and training contribute to improving human resource that is a prerequisite for an emerging economy." In order to proceed with the implementation of such development, evangelical churches are found to be key actors of quality education along side government programmes.

EVANGELICAL CHURCHES AND EDUCATION

With a majority Muslim population, Christianity accounts for a third of the country. Traditional beliefs with ancestral worship are practised by a certain number but this group is increasingly influenced by Islam and Christianity. Among the Christians there are two main groups: the Roman Catholic Church and the Protestants (Evangelicals). Christianity pioneered the early private education in Burkina Faso and the Catholic Church was also involved in higher education as well as secondary and primary. The evangelical churches initiated non-formal education well before the government and continue to bring their contribution to girls' and women's education.

Secondary school education was initially provided in schools outside Burkina Faso, as in Senegal, where the William Ponty School opened in 1915, the medical school of Dakar in 1918, and the Young Girls' School of Rufisque (Ecole Normale des Jeunes Filles) in 1939. Until 1935 Burkina Faso did not have one public secondary school. On the other hand the Roman Catholic Church opened the Seminary of Pabré in 1925 and later in 1935 the one in Koumi for the training of their priests. Their primary schools started in 1900 and the Evangelical Assemblies of God church started their primary school in 1948. These contrasts explain the reason for the low secondary school enrolment in Burkina Faso. In 1970 there was still no university and the enrolment rate for secondary education was 1.3%; in 1990 it was still only 7.5% and represented one of the lowest in Africa. There is also a huge gender gap in education. Girls are not well-represented at every level of education. In 1992-93, the girls' enrolment rate at the primary level was 24% against 37% of boys, in the rural areas this was even worse with boys' enrolment often three times higher than that of girls.

The evangelical churches in Burkina Faso are the second largest Christian body after the Roman Catholic Church. The first established churches and missions later formed the Federation of Churches and Evangelical Missions (Fédération des Eglises et Missions Evangéliques, FEME). That Federation has a dozen members, mainly from the Pentecostal background, but there are other churches that are not yet members of the Federation. All these churches share the same interest of reaching the nation with the gospel of Jesus Christ and of bringing their contribution to development issues such as health and education. They are widely represented across the nation and the Assemblies of God represents 50% of the evangelicals with about 4,000 local churches and pastors at the time of writing.

THE CASE OF THE ASSEMBLIES OF GOD CHURCH

The first believers received from the missionaries a basic training in literacy, often using the sand on the ground as a didactic tool to learn how to read and write before the Mooré alphabet was printed. Later, portions of Scripture were printed on a single sheet to memorise the verses. One verse that comes to mind is the 'Bi y tê Zu-Soaba Jesus la yãmb ne yir damb na paam fãagre' – 'Believe in the Lord Jesus, and you will be saved – you and your household' (Acts 16.31) which new Christians would have memorised. Such non-formal education took different formats of delivery but was essential to the local communities of believers. Portions of the Bible were translated by the missionaries with the help of local nationals and soon a printing press was used to print church literature.

Women learned how to read and write with the help of the American missionary ladies who trained them in special classes, at the mill, or on the way to the well to fetch water. Small Bible schools started in different regions in the main towns and villages. These different regions welcomed missionaries who were stationed there at the beginning of their field work to support with the training of the new believers and church planting initiatives.

> *Pastor Simporé was a member of the executive board of the national church of AOG. He was not sent to the first year of school because his father, who was not a Christian, forbade him to go. Simporé was recruited to the evangelical school in 1950 due to the conversion of his father to Christianity. His pastor had wanted him to come in 1948, the year the first school started in Ouagadougou. After primary school and part of secondary school in 1961 he wanted to move out and further his education elsewhere in town.*
>
> *At that stage he was contacted by Pastor Dupret requesting him to join him as a teacher. The Pastor's argument was that they should consolidate the base of education and that Simporé should join him, train as a teacher and join the staff of the school to achieve that. That suggestion was accepted and he withdrew his application to move to the national secondary school and Simporé joined the staff of the church-run school instead.*
>
> *At that time Pastor Dupret had a conviction about starting schools. He told how he received the vision from God for the schools though not all his board members agreed with him in this project, especially concerning the opening of a secondary level of education. He even showed to the eye-witnesses the place where he said God spoke to him to open the schools on that site. Pastor Dupret was convinced of this idea. Sixty years later that church influences 50% of the private evangelical schools representing 78% of the national primary education.*

The AOG church has also opened several secondary schools. Two are specifically for girls; others are mixed for general and technical studies.

It seems that God was preparing people for the future church generation. With today's progress, the church needs capable leaders. At the time the primary school was opened there were not many with high academic standards in the church apart from the American missionaries. The gospel is for all the population and the church needed more intellectuals. Those intellectuals could also reach their peer groups as well.

Today there are brothers and sisters in the church with different levels of education who can reach others both intellectually and spiritually. There are other intellectuals who did not go through the evangelical schools, but the majority of the intellectuals who impacted the church came from the evangelical schools.

> *Ibrango, a school principal in the northern region of the country, sees education as the basic tool to give instruction while at the same time sharing the gospel. In his opinion, education is the most powerful tool that has proven itself for socio-economic and spiritual development.*
>
> *When one looks in almost all the public sector, you have people that went through the evangelical schools, especially the ones founded by the AOG. All these office workers who came out of the evangelical schools are instruments of light for the gospel across the nation. You will find Christians heading government departments who are in a position to be a witness.*

Pastor Gouba, a teacher in the evangelical school since 1953, noticed that Pastor Dupret integrated girls and boys in the school.

There were no gender distinctions in his programme. He was a man with the vision. Many of these girls got married to church leaders today. The instruction they received helped them to establish harmonious families.

That church leader found his wife in the church school and got married fifty years ago. He noticed that girls' education was very necessary in the physical and in the spiritual sense. Women who are educated can help other girls learn a skill. They can also be of great help to their husbands. Non-formal education predated formal education. Chronologically, girls' and women's education came before formal schools that were started in the late 1940s.

The church put an emphasis on families from the beginning, so women were trained alongside their husbands by the wives of missionaries to learn how to read and write and assist their husbands to reach other women and girls with the gospel. This non-formal training which led to the creation of the first Bible school in Koubri, came well before the formal education of 1948. Since then eight other Bible Schools have been opened across the country for lay leadership training.

The 'Association Evangélique d'Appui au Développement' (AEAD) and speed schooling

AEAD is a national NGO which has worked in Burkina Faso since 1992. Its vision is to 'improve life through the love of God'. AEADs mission stands for creating and developing integral approaches to improve life through education, training, socio-economic development and evangelism.

In the education section of AEAD, formal and non-formal education are combined to give opportunities to children and adults to receive appropriate education in the Centre West, Centre and Northern Regions of the country. At the time of writing, AEAD were running ten formal schools reaching more than 2,000 girls and boys. A similar number are also cared for in non-formal education centres where, through adult literacy and special education programmes, men and women were exposed to an education that enables them to contribute to their own development. The last two years' reports indicate a majority of female participants

Gender in AEAD Education programmes 2008-2009

Male	Female	Total
1886 (37.5%)	3149 (62.5%)	5035

In 2006, Boulmiougou Evangelic, primary section, won the Prize of Excellence for the best primary school in the Centre region out of 667 primary schools. Similarly, the provincial Department of Education and Literacy of Zondoma sent a letter of appreciation to AEAD and considers it as an Adult Literacy Operator in the Province.

AEAD's vision has an integral approach, in the sense that it combines formal and non-formal education. It seeks to find innovative ways of working from grass-roots to fight against poverty of all sorts, whether this is economic, social or spiritual. The non-formal education allows women and men to learn how to read, write in their mother tongue and use the acquired knowledge to improve issues such as agriculture, basic health, gender, and cultural and religious values at community level.

One of the most successful ventures over the last few years has been the development of a Speed School strategy. This is aimed at those youngsters, aged 9-12, who have missed out on primary education and are thus not able to enter the national formal education schooling. An intensive, accelerated programme enables the basic three years education to be covered in nine months. It covers all the basics of mathematics, history, geography, science, civics and ethics, and entails 34 hours schooling spread over six days each week, for nine months. This has been highly successful and enabled about 90% of the children to achieve in these nine months the three years education necessary to get acceptance into a national, formal school, and thus enhance their life prospects enormously.

Number of students transferred into the formal schools 2006-2012

Number of children finishing Speed School

Boys	Girls	Total
1633	1722	3355

Number of children graduating from Speed School

Boys	Girls	Total
1440	1548	2988

So successful has this scheme been, that it was spoken of in glowing terms in the Prime Minister's Annual State of the Nation address in March 2012.

It is interesting, and encouraging, to note that the Speed Schools are in the north of Bukina Faso, which is 80% Islamic. However, this has not been an obstacle to the success of the activities in these Christian Speed Schools; indeed the Muslims are really involved and engaged in the activities of the centres, which include over 70% of the students and representation by their parents on the management committee.

THREE STORIES OF TRANSFORMATION

Mariam and Azeta

Mariam was born in 1974 in Kaksaka. She did not go to school but after her marriage went to the local church and enrolled in the literacy programme, and successfully completed both the Initial and the Basic Complementary levels. She then followed the Technical Training in hygiene, agriculture, animal husbandry and soap making. She attests that these trainings played crucial roles in transforming her life.

> I can now read the Bible, lead worship services both at church evening meetings and in my family. Administratively I serve as Vice-President of the local AEAD in the village and also as Treasurer of our local community group. I make sure that my children study well, are in good health, clean and eat well. Economically, the training allowed me to set up a small business selling cereals. These revenues help me set up a small farm with sheep and chicken. The income generated by such activities allow me to provide for my basic needs and buy school supplies for my children.

Mariam's ambitions do not stop there. She wants to expand her farming and soap business with other women. She is happy and thankful to God for giving her such opportunities. From a background of illiteracy she made her way up in the midst of a male lead culture to benefit from the literacy programme done by AEAD in the local church. Increasingly other women in the community look to her as a role model.

Azeta, who is married with two children, came from the same community as Mariam.

> I took part in the church literacy programme since 2000 and was qualified. Later on I participated in the Specific Training Programme on animal feeding and chicken poultry. In 2008 I became a literacy class teacher and received a salary that allowed me to support myself, to buy clothes, medicine and school fees for my children. As a result of my training I have three sheep and 40 chicken that generate income for me. Through the literacy programme I changed my behaviour and practice hygiene, and apply new techniques in my business. In my local church I lead the singing and often share the Word of God.

Salmata

Salmata went through AEAD Speed School programme of 2007 to discover a new life through education. She has four sisters and one brother who have not been to school. After returning from the village market her father enrolled her in the AEAD Speed School class in the village. When she was evaluated by the LEA at the end of the school year it was decided that she could jump straight to the fourth year of primary education, after completing only nine months of the accelerated method. Being the oldest among the children she is happy to be able to read, to write and do numeracy that brings hope to the whole family. She can now read letters sent to the family privately, with discretion. She is now enjoying her studies at Bethel College and intends to become a teacher to help others, especially girls and women, to improve their way of life which had previously been so restricted because of illiteracy.

Pastor Amos

In the north of Burkina Faso there is an elder of the community of a rural village who became a Christian after being first a traditional religious believer and then a Muslim. He accepted Jesus as Lord and Saviour and later became an elder in the local church in his village for many years. At the time of writing that old man is 93 years old. He served in the church development community and brought a significant transformation to his community. Now the village has access to clean water, a knowledge in farming in God's way, a village clinic initiated by the local church, a primary school open to all children of the village without discrimination, and literacy classes teaching functional languages allowing adults (especially girls and women) to improve their lives.

The elder agreed to house a church cell in his home for many years until the village pastor allowed that cell to became another local church with an additional pastor, and his family to care for the community in one part of the village. In 2012 he gave three hectares of his faming land to build the local church in one and a school in the remaining two hectares. At the time of writing that school started with one class of 55 pupils (33 boys and 22 girls) in a temporary shelter. As I write Pastor Amos is working with a builder to lay the foundation of the first classroom.

I had the opportunity to worship with that community in November 2012. That Sunday the members of the local church celebrated their harvest festival and brought into the local church building 21 bags of 100 kilogrammes each of the cereal as a joyful thanks to God. These gifts represent one tenth of the harvest from 23 households.

Conclusion

In this paper I have attempted to tell stories of transformed communities through education from Burkina Faso in West Africa. I am particularly thrilled, as the village elder referred to above, Pastor Amos, is my father. These stories are part of my Good News for you from Burkina Faso.

A Bottom-Up Perspective, for Transforming Communities

Fanen Ade

Fanen Ade is Programme Manager, Governance with Christian Aid, Nigeria. previously Senior Programme Adviser with Action Aid, Nigeria.

Introduction: Setting the Context

I grew up in an agrarian, rural community in Mbapwa, Nigeria. The local community had through self help initiatives provided such social services as roads, bridges, schools, by themselves for themselves. I am an example of a child who was able to go to school because the community established Mbaduku Community School, Tsar. This led me to work professionally in community development – first with Action Aid and subsequently with Christian Aid as senior project co-ordinator. My current research, with OCMS, is providing me with further insights into the meaning of development and the strength of social capital from the perspective of the local community.

Nigeria is a resource rich country and Africa's biggest oil producer with oil accounting for some 80% of her GDP translating to billions of dollars. In spite of Nigeria's oil wealth, the north-eastern region of Nigeria has a higher poverty rate than the poorest region of Liberia that is considered a low-income country recovering from civil war. Much aid money has been pumped into Nigeria, but little of that has got through to the distant rural communities. Most of the money seems to have been dissipated in traveling from central government, through local governments, towards the poor. Top-down development has been inefficient not only through intermediary waste but, as I increasingly believe, through an inappropriate model of development.

One of the greatest problems for rural communities in poverty is that of infant mortality and with it a pervasive sense of fatalism. It is common to hear, "The baby was meant to die" and, "It is God's will for child and woman to die" and with it, "I am poor because others made me poor. They are going to have to solve my problem. I cannot." And yet we will see that there is an alternative, there is hope.

WHAT IS COMMUNITY?

Community development is a deliberate effort by a people to come together and address a need or needs. In Mbapwa, the people saw the need for their children to acquire western education so they came together to establish community schools to meet this need. In this action the community as a unit identifies a collective need that would benefit her members. It is important to emphasise the key words of 'benefit' and 'the collective efforts' to advance a 'common good' as a bottom-up approach. These words presuppose the fact that the people (community) collectively decide what developmental issues they will advance and they commit themselves to ensuring they meet these needs. If the people as a community come up with development initiatives it is referred to as 'bottom-up' development. What this means is that the development needs of the community are 'felt' needs of the community as against externally initiated development efforts that are imposed on communities. It is easier for communities to initiate, drive, own and sustain bottom-up development initiatives because they are felt needs.

WHAT IS DEVELOPMENT?

The word development and the development process is often a construct that depicts 'top-down' approaches where governments and clever practitioners seek to make a 'less developed' place 'better'. The word 'development' often suggests an image of fixing something broken or making something better. Alkire and Deneulin (2009) wrote,

> We speak of development in many contexts like the development of a child or the development of new software as if development completes something as yet unfinished but this too is simplistic. The term development is ambiguous and value-laden and requires understanding from specific contexts.

Others conceptualise development to mean more material prosperity: having money, properties like land, houses and so on. Yet, others view development as the means to carry out a nation's development goals and promoting 'economic growth', equality and national self-reliance.

Furthermore Corbett and Fikkert (2009) in their important book *When Helping Hurts* cautioned that the way we define poverty (either implicitly or explicitly) plays a major role in determining the solution we attempt. They used the table below to summarise this:

If We believe the Primary Causes of Poverty is…	Then We Will Primarily Try to…
A Lack of Knowledge	Educate the Poor
Oppression by the Powerful People	Work for Social Justice
The Personal Sins of the Poor	Evangelise and Disciple the Poor
A Lack of Material Resources	Give Material Resources to the Poor

VOICES OF MBAPWA PEOPLE ON POVERTY AND DEVELOPMENT

In order to hear the voices of the poor, I used Focus Group Discussions (FGDs) as a method of data collection. This helps communities analyse poverty and then come up with conditions necessary for community development. These FGDs come up with what the local name(s) of 'poverty' and 'development' are and elicit interpretation and analysis of what these concepts mean to the community. It is important to note that names and naming have connotations that are onomatopoeic or metaphorical by Tiv people of Nigeria.

The Mbapwa people were asked, "What is the local name(s) for poverty and development in this community, and what is your understanding of the concepts?" They said poverty is *ichan* meaning lack, absence, or insufficiency. Another respondent quickly added that poverty is *Iban-ave.* meaning absence of what one needs at hand leading to aimlessness or purposelessness. *Iban-ave* can be closely interpreted by the adage; 'an idle man is the devils workshop', meaning when you lack what you need you become 'aimless' or purposeless'. The two words *ichan* and *iban-ave* mean the same thing literally but the interpretative meanings are descriptions of disempowerment of the poor person. Elaborating further the respondents said, "If a farmer cannot afford fertiliser for his or her farm then *Ichan* has disempowered them. So *ichan* is like an external 'force' acting to denying or depriving the farmer his or her desire to flourish." Therefore it is the inability to access farm implements like fertilisers that leads to *iban-ave* (lack). In other words, fertiliser is an external force causing *ichan*. Because if it is not accessible it is disempowering leading to *iban-ave* and ultimately aimlessness or purposelessness. So this presupposes that if the farmer gets farm inputs to farm they will improve their productivity and so *ichan* or *iban-ave* (poverty) is eliminated. Another interesting explanation to disempowerment was:

> *What you need might be there, but if you lack the purchasing power then you are poor. For instance an individual, who has a kidney problem, has the money to treat himself but if the hospital is not there he is poor. Money will not save him but if the hospital was there and he utilised his money to treat himself then that is the difference his money can make. Again, if the hospital is there but he can't afford its services he is again poor.*

Defining development was easier. After describing poverty the respondents simply said development is the opposite of poverty, which is *shagba* meaning 'wealth' or being well off or having lots of asserts. Such asserts they said could include dependants (people), food, money, clothes and so on. They explained that it was common in the past for poorer people to go to a wealthy person to borrow clothes to attend festivals or occasions. *Shagba* is also said to be the same thing as *yough-yough*, meaning 'fullness' and interpreted to mean fullness of things, self actualisation, contentment. So having people around you like children, relations, kinsmen, and extended family members means one is wealthy even if he/she does not have physical cash. A respondent elaborated,

> *Shagba is (wealthy) and if the person is a man of the people. So wealth is different from riches in terms of money. Shagba means wealth or fullness. It is like self-actualisation. A past traditional leader of the community (by name Zaki (Chief) Adedzwa Agera Akweshi) was very wealthy (man of the people, loved and liked) and so whatsoever he said was respected, adhered to and taken into consideration/account. People readily came whenever he called on them to assist him (for instance farm work, roofing of thatch huts etc.). This means he was not only wealthy (fullness or man of the people) but he was liked and accepted as a person and king.*

In the FGDs the respondents felt that the entire community was poor based on the explanations above. But I made the respondents analyse poverty deeper by coming up with categorisation of who is poor and poorest.

Poor	- Could be educated up to primary school level - Employed on a low income job e.g. night guard - Has small farm size (go to farm to enable him to gather food for his stomach and also for commercial purposes)

| | - Can afford to sponsor their children up to post primary school level
| | - Has food to eat and food could contain fish or meat
| | - Can pay medical bills (but not in a sophisticated hospital)
| | - Has a house (thatched/zinc roof)
| Poorest | - Has no land
| | - Has no wife (has a family he does not take care of – such children could become nuisance)
| | - Has no house (may be living in a dilapidated room given to him by a friend)
| | - Cannot afford medical bills
| | - Cannot pay taxes
| | - Has no farm of his own (feeds from other people's homes, he is more or less a parasite or beggar)
| | - Is extremely lazy
| | - Does not keep his plates tidy
| | - Often steals foodstuff from other people's farm.

From this the working definition of poverty was agreed by the respondents as, "lack of and obstacle to attaining fullness (*shagba, yough-yough*) including access to basic needs like food, water, shelter, clothing and healthcare." Development on the other hand was said to be the opposite of poverty and summed up to be "the opportunities available to all humans to attain fullness."

CONDITIONS THAT WOULD SUPPORT INDIVIDUAL AND COMMUNITY DEVELOPMENT

The Mbapwa people said values are at the centre of what makes people pursue what they want and value. However, to enable respondents to analyse more rigorously, they were given a hypothetical case study of four children (two boys and two girls) born on the same day. The task for the respondents was to list the conditions as to why one of the children became rich while the others may remain poor or very poor. The respondents said parents have varying backgrounds, exposure, and financial standing. They said it also depends on the extent to which parents make efforts to instil in their children good community values like hard work, commitment and honesty. However, the respondents said if the children are of the same parents the difference could be because some children spend more time playing around rather than being hard working and determined.

The respondents suggested factors supporting human development which fell into two categories: firstly, those factors within the control of the individual (internal) and secondly, those outside the immediate control of the individual (external). Internal categories included hard working, determination and resource management; external categories included inadequate farm land, fertiliser, and lack of education. The conditions external to the individual are the opportunities needed by the individual to enable the attainment of 'fullness'. The external conditions are causalities that could produce fullness including 'access' and 'opportunity'. Some conditions that support community development are external and the individual has little or no control over them. Therefore there is need for a higher regulatory system to minimise the impact of these external conditions and their potential to drive and or cause poverty.

It is interesting to note that most external conditions required to support the individual and community development are beyond the capability of the agent (individual). In this way the individual could be hard working and determined but can be limited by these external conditions. The community members said a hard working child from Mbapwa community determined to be a surgeon could be limited by poor access to quality education or poor sponsorship as external factors. The summary of the general community expressed was:

> *Some children lack sponsorship and help. If only they had someone to pay for their education, they will not be failures. It is true that committed persons went to school in spite of the distance but the others too would have received an education if the government brought schools closer to our locality.*

The understanding of what communities value could go a long way to support the kind of development initiatives to embark upon by the government. The ability of the state to achieve its objectives depends on its legitimacy and confidence of the citizens in policies of the government. This depends so much on internal cohesion, economic conditions and most importantly the degrees of social mobilisation. For instance, *Tyo hemba* and *Or hembe tyo ga* amongst the Tiv people means 'community is supreme'. This defines how these people reason and shows the flow of social contract and accountability. *Tyo hemba* is an accountability pronouncement that placed an obligation on and is binding between the individual, family and community as interacting entities. The respondents said the community had, and still has, an obligation over extended and nuclear families and the individual and there is interdependence amongst them.

For the Mbapwa people, community is the most powerful and influential entity in their lives, followed by the extended and nuclear families, and lastly the individual. Communities defined development and the conditions necessary for individual and community development. Therefore this process of development is building consensus based on the institutions, values and accountability mechanism of the community, and managing dissent.

In Nigeria the scale of issues community development needs to grapple with are considerable. From my experience, bottom-up development efforts built on community initiatives are sustained and thrive better than top-down and externally initiated development interventions. Development needs to get answers or solutions to the real problems faced by the poor wherever they are. Rural communities have initiated and successfully supported themselves through self-help initiatives in the absence, and inability, of the government of Nigeria to provide social services.

ONMBAYAAV WIDOWS MULTIPURPOSE COOPERATIVE SOCIETY (OWMCS)

The OWMCS is based in Mbapwa. The inhabitants are predominantly subsistence farmers, blacksmiths and hunters. OWMCS is a community-based self-help micro credit association. These groups of widows came together in the 1990s to establish the association as response to the increasing numbers of widows in the community and their vulnerability to deepening levels of poverty. The widows group sought and entered into partnership with Emmanuel Maikur Ade (EMA) Development Foundation, a local charity in Nigeria. EMA in turn engaged the services of Anglican Diocesan Development Services (ADDS), with years of experience in micro-credit and organisational development to train the women. The trainings were also a learning process for both partnering organisations to build trust and learn the cultural and political sensitivities of the community.

The work with the first widows group by EMA and the Anglican diocese of Makurdi commenced in year 2006. Since then, the first widows group has been able to scale up their work to three more villages. The group has also given sub-grants to the other three new widows groups to commence independent operations. The work by the widows groups has allowed women that are not yet widows to also join and become members of the widows group. Some of their achievements amongst others include:

- The first widows group has 46 members and has given out revolving loans to all her members with testimonies of how the loans have supported their farm work, school fees and care for their orphaned children.
- This first widows group has built an office complex for their work and operations though direct labour.
- The first widows group has established a second widows group with a membership of 90 women.
- The second widows group has established a third widows group in 2012 with a membership of over 30 women.
- A fourth widows group of 25 women has also been established in 2012 by the first widows group.
- The women of the fourth women group heard of the successes of the micro-credit scheme and travelled to Mbapwa to ask the first widows group to extend the scheme to their village.
- All the four women's groups have bank accounts, books of account for income and expenditure, a constitution for operation, are registered with the local authorities, and keep records of individual group meetings and deliberations.
- Another requirement for establishing a group is recognition by the traditional and religious authorities. This is both an advocacy strategy to get the support of men and entire community members for the scheme. This is also to ensure that community support will be given in the event defaulters fail to repay the loans, and the community mediation and loan recovery mechanism will be deployed.

LEARNING AND LESSONS FROM THE WORK WITH THE WIDOWS' GROUP

After further work with the women's group the following lessons were highlighted;

- Community has a structure and pattern and knowing this pattern and structure was extremely important to the work with the widows.
- As development practitioners we saw the community as a homogeneous whole but we were soon to learn that the communities have patterns and borders based on their lineages and kinship.
- The emphasis was on 'community' and on social interaction as the inherent and indispensable ingredient of community. The success of any development endeavour with rural communities is dependent on understanding the network of relationships, interactions and patterns of affinities they hold. These patterns of affinity confer identity, belongings and shared sense of purpose. These patterns of identity are seen as development in itself and are held higher than any presupposed development outcome.
- We learnt that Mbaduku as a district has two kindreds (Mbatyogh and Nyimagbagh) and each kindred has a kindred head. Nyimagbagh kindred where the work with the widows took place has three clans (each clan has a clan head). Finally, the Onmbayaagh sub-clan were the work took place has four *ngo* (meaning mothers), Mbayaav is one of the mothers and Mbayaav is where the initial micro-credit programme began. For any practitioner, learning and understanding these pattern makes his or her work more acceptable.
- The structuring of the micro-credit initiative along the community pattern with the women retained their interactional network, affinities and quality.

Any attempt to lump all rural communities into a homogeneous whole has always been met with resistance. This confrontation between rural communities and development practitioners has lead to the classification of rural communities as traditionalist resisting modernisation. The secularisation theory which assumes that when modernity advances traditional forms of social organisation including religious ones will recede has failed. These assumptions lead to the neglect of rural informal institutions such as norms, values and religious beliefs, hoping they will become extinct and die a natural death. The emergence of, or movements to, colonize supposedly 'empty territories' and establish new empires and states did not take into consideration peculiarities like values and institutions of the colonizing places. State building and 'development' was therefore not embedded.

MISSION WORK AND OTHER SELF-HELP INITIATIVES WITHIN MBAPWA

Mbapwa community, a border community around the Cameroon Mountains, is far from the seat of government and is largely 'forgotten'. Agera Akweshi established a church and school when he became a Christian with *Nongu u Kristu u ken Sudan hen Tiv* (NKST). NKST is a reformed mission church translated to mean 'Church of Christ in the Sudan Among the Tiv'. Therefore, western education in Mbapwa has its roots from mission work after the acceptance of Christianity by the locals.

In Nigeria it is these lagging forms of traditionalism like religious institutions, traditional leadership and community development associations, that serve as support systems and supply social services. Where the 'modern' state has failed community associations provide local governance, social control and social services. These traditional institutions tend to serve rural people better and have more legitimacy and authority than the state in Nigeria. The churches already have respected organisations, and their actions are perceived as less politically driven and selfish than those of the government, which are not well trusted.

The 'absence' of state and its inability to provide social amenities has made religious organisations and a few well-meaning individuals providers of social services. These services include schools, community policing and security, social care, safety nets, community development projects and so on. But for missionaries and other community development initiatives, rural communities like Mbapwa and many like them would not have had western education. Traditional rulers and missionaries enjoy and trade on the currency of trust, legitimacy and authority as the 'only' recognised governance systems. There is deficit of trust for government and citizens view government pronouncements with suspicion and distrust.

LESSONS AND CHALLENGES

The curiosity to understand what community development comes from these rural communities led me to collect and analyse data from Mbapwa community to know their own perception of community development. In the process I learnt two lessons. Firstly, the table above by Corbett and Fikkert (see p.95) was the way I was conditioned by my training as a development practitioner to see and think about poor people and community development. But now I am reflecting and stepping back to ask myself whether it is not better to listen more to the voices of the communities themselves. Secondly, from my experience working as a development practitioner, I am developing a thesis that community, institutions and their values determine the development, wellbeing and happiness of its members. From this I am increasingly coming to two conclusions.

- Firstly, what people value and their institutions should be respected and accepted as their development.
- Secondly, anytime the word 'development' is written it should be put in inverted comas until the 'development experts' listen to what rural people want as their development.

Another problem is the operation of the community and her institutions and values within the legal framework and constitution of the nation state. How do we as 'development' practitioners balance between government 'development' priorities and the priorities of rural communities? To what extent can these very different authorities complement each other?

Farmers are vulnerable to market uncertainties and the condition of the poor has deteriorated further because governments across the African continent are compelled to cut public expenditures. These restrictions are part of an International Monetary Fund (IMF) and World Bank economic restructuring programs known as Structural Adjustment Programme (SAP). In Northern Nigeria, the encroachment of the Sahara Desert means that rural farmers are losing farmlands to desertification requiring the construction of dams for irrigated farming. The farmers need farm inputs like fertilisers to support farming activities and pregnant women need good medical facilities and qualified personnel. Rural communities enjoy a huge stock of social capital and networks, but the realities faced by individuals like child-bearing women and the farmers in

Northern Nigeria is beyond these poor people's resources, and requires government intervention.

The women need primary healthcare facilities to avoid maternal deaths and minimise child mortality rate or prevent avoidable deaths. The implementation of IMF and World Bank policies based on neoclassical economics proposed that the economic role of the state should be minimised: the state should be 'rolled back'. The economy should be left to the price mechanisms in competitive markets to decide what should be produced and in what quantities. In this approach, excess produced in the cause of perfectly competitive markets is assumed to be rationally distributed and will trickle down to the poor leading to economic growth and development. In the last three decades of implementing these IMF and World Bank policies poverty has increased in Nigeria. Downscaled state intervention means rural communities like Mbapwa will continue to exist without healthcare facilities or post-primary schools. This will inevitably lead to the death of pregnant women without prenatal, antenatal and postnatal care, resulting in more maternal deaths and child mortality. Thus a gap has been created between the government's objectives and the people's value system as the main obstacles to participation in rural development.

CONCLUSION

More often than not development is treated as something outside and superior to what already exists within and amongst the community. The downscaled role of the state has made community development initiatives the most notable expression of citizenship and development endeavours. The development alternative in Africa is the recognition of her stock of social capital as reality that needs utilising. The difficulty in comprehending community and social capital does not justify wishing it away as traditionalism resistant to hubris. Focusing efforts on community and the interactional approach will unveil the networks and outcomes rural communities cherish that equates as development. The networks and relationships within communities form safety nets and support systems for vulnerable and less able community members in times of shock and need. The social exchanges community members enter into produces outcomes that support their wellbeing, happiness and shared existence in the absence of social care and support by government.

CARING FOR OUR SISTERS, COMFORTING THE ABUSED

JENNIFER SINGH

Jennifer Singh is Project Officer Samaritan's Purse, Uganda and Ethiopia, and was previously with International Christian Alliance on Prostitution (ICAP) in Cambodia.

THE PROBLEM

While serving with Hagar International and Samaritan's Purse in Cambodia between 2001 and 2005, human-trafficking was a term that started to be increasingly used within the wider NGO community as accounts began to emerge of girls as young as four years-old being stolen from their parents, and confined in brothels to be repeatedly raped by men. It did not seem to matter what sector one was working in as stories of human-trafficking began to be reported by agencies engaged in a wide spectrum of humanitarian work ranging from clean water to women's projects. The risk-factors leaving girls, women, and young boys vulnerable to sexual exploitation through human-trafficking (e.g. poverty, gender inequality, lack of clean water and nutritious food etc.) spanned every sector which worked to 'raise the alarm' on this horrific issue.

As a result, in Asia significant public attention and NGO interventions have since been undertaken with regards to human-trafficking, for the purpose of sexual exploitation which has been defined as "recruiting, harbouring, transporting, providing, or obtaining a person for a commercial sex-act that is induced by force, fraud, or coercion." However, girls and women are being sexually exploited through human-trafficking at alarming rates all over the world, including Africa. The International Labour Organisation's 2012 Global Estimate of Forced Labour Report estimates that of the 20.9 million people currently being victimised through human-trafficking, 3.7 million of those are found in Africa (18%) and that the African prevalence rate of 4.0 victims per 1000 inhabitants, represents the second highest regional prevalence rate in the world.

I was exposed to the reality of this statistic during my first visit to Ethiopia in 2009 while serving with the International Christian Alliance on Prostitution (ICAP), a global network of Christian practitioners committed to offering restorative care to victims of prostitution and human-trafficking. Serawit (Cherry) Teketel Friedmeyer is the Africa Regional Director of ICAP and also the founder of Ellilta Women at Risk (EWAR), a ministry partner of Samaritan's Purse, a grassroots Christian organisation based in Addis Ababa that has in the past 15 years assisted over 500 women out of a life of prostitution. EWAR seeks-out intentional friendship and trust with women currently in prostitution as a first step in introducing them to their fuller ministry.

Cherry and her team introduced me to the horror of the situation in Ethiopia where, in Addis Ababa alone, it is estimated that over 150,000 women are in prostitution. Driving through the red-light districts of the capital city, and seeing row-upon-row of women lined up against the wall outside the central bus station, standing shyly with their heads wrapped in scarves, and girls barely past their adolescence awkwardly interacting with men much their senior in dark alleys, shocked, disgusted, and ruined me all at the same time.

I was *shocked* by the sheer volume of women on the streets and could not imagine that there was enough 'demand' for such a plentiful 'supply' but I came to quickly learn that the primary reason that the global sex-industry is thriving is because of the demand: If there was no demand, there would not be any supply. I was *disgusted* to see how these women were being solicited with complete impunity by men much larger in stature and older in age. The physical, emotional, and social vulnerability of these women was so patently obvious to even the most casual of observers, and the thin scarves they wore were a visible symbol of the lack of protection and dignity they had. I was *ruined* in the sense that after bearing witness to such evil, such dehumanisation, I would never be the same again. These women were no longer statistics, but image-bearers of the Most High God, faces with names and stories of indescribable suffering – they were *my sisters*.

This realisation was only confirmed throughout the rest of my time in Ethiopia after seeing how the counselling, discipleship, child-development and vocational training programs that EWAR offers to eighty women per year was serving to completely transform these women, to *humanize* them. These women who had once been reduced to ascribing their value to how many Birr (local currency) they could earn in one evening, are now able to run small-businesses, to pay for the children's school fees, to worship God in local congregations, and most importantly, to look in the mirror and see themselves as made in the image of God with a worth and value that is priceless.

THE SOLUTION

The compassionate care of the EWAR staff, the family atmosphere they create, and the grace-saturated context in which they serve these women are just some of the factors that have worked to help over 500 women and their children to exit a life of prostitution over the past 15 years. These women have been able to receive deep healing and restoration, which in turn has empowered them to overcome their trauma and to pursue livelihood opportunities that have allowed them to build loving and stable homes for their children. For EWAR, success is measured by the ability of a woman never to return to the streets, and in their 15 year history, they have experienced a 94% success rate: 94% of the women who have gone through their programme go on to lead dignified and sustainable lives. In addition, several of these women that have gone through the programme are now serving in key leadership positions at EWAR – evidence of the kingdom breaking-in and transformation occurring.

EWAR has become a model of holistic restorative ministry to prostituted women in Africa, and as a result, has been sought-out over the last five years by 16 Christian, grassroots organisations from across Africa that are reaching-out to prostituted women. In partnership with Samaritan's Purse, EWAR has been offering an online training programme designed to help build the organisational, theological, and programmatic capacity of these programs, and have focused teaching on specific areas of need as identified by these organisations, such as Christian counselling and church mobilisation.

However, one of the greatest challenges these organisations have encountered, whether it has been in Addis Ababa, Ouagadougou, or Durban, has been the reticence and sometimes outright hostility of the church in their local context to become engaged in this work with the women. One of these organisations that EWAR has been a 'midwife to' in Uganda, and has slowly begun to overcome some of the entrenched stigmas, attitudes, and misguided beliefs, has been Sanyuka Women at Risk (SWAR).

Sanyuka was first conceived in the heart of its founder, Mary Zema, who had lived the life of a prostituted woman for eleven years, travelling the main trucking route from Mombasa to Kampala, trying to provide for herself and her family. Mary had fallen into prostitution as a result of the death of her father and the neglect and abuse she suffered at the hands of her mother, which eventually led to her fleeing to the streets at a young age. Mary was sexually abused and from this experience quickly learned that the only way to survive on the streets and have some semblance of control over her life and body was to engage in prostitution. Her story is filled with tragedies that most of us reading this would not be able to comprehend, which eventually led her to the point of desiring to take her own life.

On the night she had planned to commit suicide, a Christian couple walked into the bar where she was working due to a 'coincidental' vehicle break-down in front of the bar. The couple took one look at the deep sadness etched on Mary's face and said: "God loves you, God wants to take care of your family, and God has a plan for your life." Mary collapsed on the ground and began to weep in a way that she had not before, over all of the painful years of her life. The couple bore witness to Mary's pain and prayed with Mary to receive Jesus Christ as her Lord and Saviour on the bar floor.

The next morning, a pastor of a local church encountered Mary sleeping on the steps of church where she had spent the rest of the night. "Pastor, I need help," were the first words that came from Mary, to which he responded, "What is this?" The pastor and his staff struggled to believe the story they were hearing, and said, "If you have really accepted Christ in your life, then you will come back here in three days and then we will help you." Mary left the church distraught and hopeful all at the same time, returned to the brothel where she was living, got rid of all of her belongings, and sat in a park and began to weep... for the entire three days. Mary never grew cold or hungry in those three days where the Lord began to heal Mary through her tears of pain and grief over the life she had lived. Mary returned to the church, much to the surprise of the staff, and after being given shelter for one week, the assistant pastor dropped her off at the Youth With A Mission (YWAM) base in Mombasa and left her there without even saying goodbye. Unlike the church, the YWAM community instantly believed and embraced Mary's story and she was invited to join them and spent several years being healed by a loving community, discipled in the Word of God, and trained in how to initiate a pioneering ministry.

Mary eventually transferred to a YWAM located close to Jinja, Uganda, which neighbours Mbiko, one of the major truck-stop towns found on the highway between Nairobi and Kampala. As characteristic of 'truck-stop' towns, Mbiko is lined with bars, brothels, and single-bed abodes to house men for a few hours while they take a short break on their long journeys. On any given night, one can find dozens of tractor-trailers lined up alongside the highway, and the drivers revelling in the anonymity that their job affords them as they pursue the plentiful vice-filled opportunities that a town like Mbiko can offer.

During Mary's process of rehabilitation, friends that were still on the streets and struggling with the lifestyle she had found freedom from, still haunted Mary. "If only they could find the freedom that I have," was a thought constantly on Mary's mind. She wanted to do something for these women, and being located so closely to Mbiko, Mary found herself increasingly in friendships with women who were working in the bars and caught-up in prostitution. Mary barely had enough of an income through her jewellery business to make ends meet for her own family, much less discretionary funds, but she knew she had to respond to the plight of the women in her community who she closely identified with, and saw as her sisters.

In a huge leap of faith, Mary began to frequent the Mbiko bar-scene, offering friendship and hope to the women there: Mary wanted these women to know that they were heard and seen by God, and that God could do in their lives what he had done in hers. She initiated Bible-studies in the bars and soon women would be meeting her at the bar entrances saying, "Auntie Mary, Auntie Mary, when are you coming back? Can you help us out of this life?" These women saw something different about Mary during her nightly visits: she did not hurl demeaning words at them, she did not use a Bible as a sword to pierce at the wounds of shame these women had endured through this dehumanizing trade, she did not ignore them or treat them as objects. Mary condescended in the same manner as our Loving Lord and met these women where they were at – in the red-light district – in their brokenness, pain, and desperation, and offered them a relationship with someone who cared. Friendship is one of the most humanizing vehicles that the Lord ever modelled for, "Greater love has no one than this: to lay down one's life for one's friends" (John 15:13).

THE CHALLENGE OF ENGAGING THE LOCAL CHURCH
Thus began the ministry of Sanyuka where in the past five years, over 40 women and their children have been able to realise freedom from a life of prostitution. In the early days of the ministry, Mary opened-up her home and began to house a number of these women but quickly realised that food and shelter were not enough to heal the deep wounds and scars these women had endured: they needed a structured environment where trauma could be processed, discipleship could occur, livelihood skills could be taught, and the children of these women could be cared for. It was at this point that Mary's life intersected with EWAR, and she began making an annual 'pilgrimage' to Addis Ababa in order to learn from the staff, women, and program. The EWAR team took Mary under their wing and imparted as much of their collective wisdom as they could, while simultaneously advocating with several of their own donors to provide Mary with the chance to start a centre similar to EWAR in Mbiko.

Mary would faithfully try to implement the organisational, financial, and programmatic teachings she would receive on these annual trips to Addis, all the while continuing to support a number of women living in her home trying to leave prostitution through her meagre jewellery-making income. One important lesson Mary had learned from her 'older sister' in Ethiopia was that once these women found healing, they would need communities of faith to support them, but in the context of Addis Ababa, that had been one of the greatest challenges EWAR had encountered. When women in their programme were ready for baptism, EWAR would approach local congregations and, in the early days, none of them would permit the service in their churches for fear of "those women contaminating our congregations" and an inherent belief that these women were not "clean enough" to accept the life of Christ. Finding a place to baptise born-again believers was a problem to the church in Addis!

Mary was determined not to have the women she was journeying with experience the kind of rejection, discrimination, and gracelessness that had marked the early days of EWAR's church engagement and set-out to build intentional relationships with the churches in the Mbiko area. When Mary would share the stories of the women she knew and the work of Sanyuka, she was met with a lot of admiration and respect by church leaders for working with 'those' women and words of support: "tell us what we can do… how can we help? …we will pray for you…." Sanyuka began to organise sensitisation trainings with local church congregations in order to start answering these questions, and emphasised the vital role that local churches had in offering a family and community to these women who had lived as despised outcasts in society. Sanyuka appealed to the story of the Good Samaritan where the victim left for dead on the side of the road was embraced by the Samaritan, who did not fear the messiness and danger that the victim's situation presented in that moment. Instead, he rolled-up his sleeves and began to administer the costly elements of oil and wine to the injured man in order to start a process of deep healing in his life.

Despite the compelling case for these women that Sanyuka was making to these churches, based on biblical truths and living testimonies of women experiencing transformation through the program, it was not enough to motivate the churches to action. The churches were definitely welcoming to women going through the programme attending their Sunday services but, in terms of intentionally discipling, following-up, and counselling these women, the churches were devoid of interest. Sanyuka had approached local congregations in the hope that they could fill the need for family, community and belonging that these women desperately required as a part of their healing process. Vision-bearers (e.g. senior pastors and elders) of the churches they had met with had wholeheartedly expressed agreement with this idea but seemed unable (or unwilling) to implement the practical measures necessary to ensuring this would happen.

Intentionality was at the heart of the message Sanyuka was trying to convey to the local congregations. All too often they had seen women from the programme shyly slinking into a Sunday service late to avoid the awkwardness of the 'meet and greet', sitting in the very back row, and rushing out before the last prayer was uttered in order to avoid the danger of being recognised [by her former life] as one of the girls standing on the side of the road. Local congregations failed to understand the incredible amount of courage and vulnerability it takes for a formerly prostituted woman to step into the 'house of God' after spending so many years being characterised as the 'chief of sinners' by society at large.

It is extremely difficult for one to understand the incredible amount of shame that formerly prostituted women bear, and walking into a place like a church can often serve to only heighten that sense of disgrace, uncleanness, and otherness that these women feel in every fibre of their being.

In the brilliant exposition of the Beatitudes (Matthew 6) that Dietrich Bonhoeffer provides in *The Cost of Discipleship*, he speaks about the role of the local church as coming alongside the broken and bearing the weight of their sin and shame. He says it is not enough for the Body of Christ to offer a word of absolution to those that have existed in a broken relationship to God, but as a community, to inhabit that shame together and to bring it to the foot of the Cross so that the shamed one can be reconciled to their God. "Blessed are the merciful for they shall receive mercy". The ministry of mercy requires bearing the shame and brokenness of our sisters, and incarnating the pursuing heart of the Father. In the story of the Prodigal Son, the father saw his son "from a long way off... ran to his son, threw his arms around him and kissed him" (Luke 15:21). The response of the Prodigal Son to the abundant mercy offered by his father, "I am no longer worthy to be called your son" echoes the cry of formerly prostituted women stepping into a local congregation and must be met with the same response of the father who tells his servants to "bring the best robe and put it on him... let's have a feast and celebrate. For this son of mine was dead and is alive again, he was lost and is found" (Luke 15:22-24). Local congregations must work intentionally to pursue, clothe, embrace, and celebrate the homecoming of our sisters in order to remove the bondage of shame they have lived in for so long, and to experience the healing and restoration that only a community can provide.

In the quest to find places where intentional community would be pursued with the women, Sanyuka began to focus its teaching and awareness training on women within local congregations. The Sanyuka team were convinced that the women they were working with needed travelling companions on their salvation journey, and that older and wise women within local congregations could be compelled to act as a 'Spiritual Mother' to the women. The basic criteria to become a Spiritual Mother was a demonstrated attitude of compassion toward prostituted women, knowledge of the word, and the willingness to avail their time to disciple these women as they took their first tentative steps into the new life they were pursuing.

One of the greatest challenges that women trying to exit prostitution face is the temptation to fall back into their old lifestyle. Still being physically located close to the red-light areas, and with an overwhelming sense of unworthiness and lack of self-esteem, and with big financial constraints, they feel there is nothing else they can do with their life.

Sanyuka realised that Spiritual Mothers could act like a 'sponsor' in the Alcoholics Anonymous programme, encouraging the women in their greatest moments of weakness and temptation, being a much needed listening ear as they navigate the multitude of challenges faced as the sole bread-winner of the family, and speaking truth and love into their life on a consistent basis. Women in various congregations expressed interest in becoming Spiritual Mothers and after some training with them, Sanyuka was able to match several women in the programme with these new spiritual guides. Currently, this aspect of the programme is being further developed and expanded, and Sanyuka has seen how the intentional care of the Spiritual Mothers has worked to incarnate the radical hospitality and unconditional love of Christ to the women in the program. Spiritual Mothers are community 'brokers' in many ways as they liaise between their local congregations and the needs of the women. The intentional relationships being initiated by the Spiritual Mothers are like the entranceway of the local congregation through which the women are able to step through, without the fear of condemnation and rejection.

Lessons Learned

Through journeying alongside organisations like EWAR and Sanyuka, Samaritan's Purse has learned that we can play a vital bridging role between grassroots ministries responding to the plight of prostituted women, and local congregations where these issues are occurring. The work of individuals in local grassroots organisations is an example to the institutional church that must be lauded, upheld, and supported both at a spiritual and material level by local congregations. The mission statement of Samaritan's Purse states that "the organisation serves the church worldwide in order to promote the gospel of Jesus Christ." Fulfilling this mandate in ministry to prostituted women would be to see more local congregations rising-up to the challenge of providing preventative and restorative measures to ensure that the exploitation of women through this dehumanizing trade ends.

To this end, Samaritan's Purse in Uganda has initiated work on one of the islands on Lake Victoria where prostitution is rampant due to the transient nature of the fishing industry which dominates the island. Men are drawn to the island to fish, and sadly fall prey to the high levels of alcoholism that prevail as drinking is the main activity pursued by the fishermen when not working on the lake. Women come to the island often to start 'drinking joints' as a result of the high demand for alcohol, but quickly find themselves providing 'services' that are also in high demand: prostitution. Samaritan's Purse is working to bring a biblical and theological framework to local churches on the island that includes prostituted women amongst the category of the vulnerable in order that churches will begin to practically respond to the plight of these women. Local churches have demonstrated polite curiosity to date, but we still have a long way to go in convincing them that these women are God's image bearers in desperate need of restoration. One pastor recently told us, "If I go to those areas where those women are [the red-light districts], the gospel will be ruined, ruined." Comments like these are indicative of the depth of stigma that needs to be unearthed and categorically dealt with so that local congregations are freed from the bondage of judgementalism and empowered to work collaboratively in order to see more of God's kingdom realised in this very dark reality.

In order to respond directly to these potent stigmas that often serve as barriers to churches becoming involved in ministry to prostituted women, Samaritan's Purse Uganda began a new initiative in 2013 called 'My Sister's Keeper' because of our conviction that every single woman in prostitution today could be our mother, friend, daughter, sister…we are all our 'sister's keeper'. This project is designed to directly dismantle these stigmatizing beliefs and to equip the local Body of Christ to take responsibility for our sisters by: inspiring, mobilising, equipping and strengthening the capacity of seven local Ugandan churches, to prevent vulnerable girls and women from being sexually exploited, and to practically respond to the needs of those seeking to flee abusive and exploitative situations.

KEY LESSONS LEARNED
- The first and greatest 'resource' the local Body of Christ has to offer to a prostituted women is their time – relationships are the key to helping women believe they can exit this lifestyle and the fellowship and family that a local congregation can offer to women who have been so marginalised, cannot be underestimated in terms of its power to heal and transform.
- We, as the church, need to reckon and deal with our stigmas and fears towards reaching out to prostituted women before we can approach these women with any sincerity and genuineness – they will be able to discern if our motivation if fuelled by condemnation or genuine compassion.
- The church has great potential for becoming involved in this particular issue, not only through restoring those that have fallen victim but in also preventing this horrible exploitation from happening through recognizing and addressing the *root causes* that make women vulnerable to prostitution. The word of God is one of the most powerful tools we have to start addressing the deep-seated values that perpetuate patriarchy, misogyny, and other harmful beliefs that far too often relegate women to less than human status.
- The church must be willing to deal with the 'demand-side' in this equation of exploitation and to address the lie that sex is a commodity that can be bought and sold on the open-market. Men in local congregations must be lovingly challenged about their concepts of masculinity and be willing to engage in a discipleship process that re-envisions a masculinity that includes attitudes and behaviours that honour and respect women, and are committed to having this transferred into the fathering practices for the next generation. The hope is that these Christian men will serve as role-models to the entire community at large.

OUTSTANDING ISSUES
- The perception by the church that the overwhelming needs of women trying to exit a life of prostitution (e.g. counselling,

livelihood, childcare etc.) are 'too much' for them to handle. Many Ugandan churches feel short of resources and therefore believe they do not have the means to truly help these women 'out' of this exploitation.
- Moving the dialogue out of the realm of 'sin/salvation' issues (prostitution is not simply the result of making bad/sinful choices) and the church being able to recognise this as a *justice issue*, one that the church must be willing to identify with and come against.
- Church leaders struggle to really believe that prostituted women can experience transformation and really 'exit' this lifestyle – they lack hope, thus this project will seek to give a tangible example of this hope by connecting local congregations with local grassroots ministries that have facilitated women coming to know Jesus Christ as their saviour, deliverer, healer and provider – women who have experienced the kingdom being realised in their lives, as it is in heaven.

CONCLUSION

Uganda has been described as the pearl of Africa. Jesus has been described as the pearl of great price. Can the church in seeing Jesus in these prostituted women, become willing, able, and ready to pursue them, to find them in the darkness and companion with them into the light, to help restore the Image of God that the Lord has intended for them to so beautifully bear, and to risk everything – relished beliefs, reputation, resources – to ensure that these precious 'pearls' are redeemed and written into the Lamb's Book of Life?

Conclusions and Outstanding Issues
Brian Woolnough

We started this discussion with the recognition that not all aid leads to sensible, sustainable development – indeed that some aid actually does harm. In the subsequent chapters we have seen examples of good practice, where the communities have genuinely benefited. In each case the development has been bottom-up, community lead, church based, and holistic. In particular we have seen examples of Tearfund's approach, working through and with the local churches, with strategies such as Umoja and the earlier CCMP. There has been a consistency of 'listening to the poor'.

We have seen stories bringing 'good news from Africa' and whilst recognising that there is still much need, much poverty, much injustice and inequality in Africa, we should acknowledge that there has been much progress across the 54 countries in Africa. Infant mortality is down, and health generally improved. HIV/AIDS is being controlled, if not resolved. Universal education, including girls, has been widely recognised. Economically, many countries are showing remarkable growth, largely though not entirely through better use of natural resources such as oil. Politically, whilst there is still much bad governance in many countries, others have adopted genuinely democratic governance, and some even have women prime-ministers! For many, living standards and opportunities have improved considerably.

It is debateable however whether the individual and community well-being has grown in parallel with the material and financial growth. Many communities have been broken up, partly through resource exploitation and partly through social mobility to the towns and cities, and with that has been the loss of community values and the traditional extended family. The church in Africa has demonstrated wonderful growth, though even here the church's effectiveness is being attacked by an excessive emphasis on materialist and prosperity values and, in some areas, a resurgent Islamic militancy. But genuine development there has been over the last few decades.

WHAT DO WE MEAN BY DEVELOPMENT?
Whose development is being promoted? So often still the aid being proffered is top-down, with associations of the western, secular society, driven by a materialistic agenda. Even with Christian NGOs the strategies are often determined by the donor's priorities, and come with the cultural attributes of the donor's national traditions. Is it not possible to be more sensitive to the recipient's culture, and their understanding of, and preferences in, development? In the west we concentrate on individualist, material gain. Many majority world cultures prefer communal, relational, and holistic development, expecting spiritual as well as material transformation.

It is clear that much top-down aid (a) gets dissipated through governments and intermediaries, and (b) causes dependency in the receptor because of the expense of maintaining western style technology and economic structures. Irene, Fanen and Donald stressed the need 'to listen to the poor' to ensure that a more appropriate form of development is targeted; Fanem especially stresses the need for bottom-up development.

Must the 'piper always call the tune'? Is it possible for donor organisations to genuinely listen to the poor, to hear them, and then act altruistically in accord with those wishes? Donald, through Umoja, asserts yes.

HOW DOES OUR THEOLOGY AFFECT OUR AIMS AND STRATEGY?
Underlying the motives and methods of development workers lies fundamental issues of world-view. A secular agency will concentrate on the material aspects of development. Christians have, particularly in the past, been split into those who prioritise the saving of souls and those who seek to provide physical help and relief. The theology which claims that God's love and God's good news is holistic, necessitating both material and spiritual development, will have a different emphasis.

Most Christian NGOs now profess a holistic gospel, but there are still variations in practice. Some ignore the physical needs of those they seek to save. Some lose sight of the spiritual needs in the practicalities of delivering physical relief. How can we ensure that we are genuinely delivering a holistic gospel? The answer must be that by working through the local church we have within the church the full range of aims, both to

Conclusions and Outstanding Issues

save and disciple the soul and to care for the physical and emotional needs of the poor. It is only working through and with the local church that both aspects of transformational development can be delivered.

Such theological perspectives permeate all our work, indeed all our lives. What does God want of us? WWJD? To demonstrate his love to those in need. Full stop. I have seen Kenneth's work in Uganda and been impressed by their workers' T-shirts boldly proclaiming 'Water is life, Jesus is everlasting life', a statement of holistic theology which permeates their whole approach. A Christian nurse in Mumbai, when asked why she had spent so much time and effort on a dying, unresponsive, woman answered, "Well, obviously. God is love and she needed love." Full stop!

What then is the difference between the work of a Christian NGO and a secular NGO? There are obvious and important differences, related to the motivation, the prayer support, the priorities, and the dependence on the Holy Spirit. But the remarkable concept of *Missio Dei*, that God is at work throughout the whole world, through Christians and non-Christians too, should enable Christian and secular NGOs to celebrate each others' work, though only a CNGO will be able to work for holistic transformation.

Theological questions about the nature and the purpose of the church – to worship God or to serve the community – will also affect how much the church perceives the need to help the needy. A 'gathered flock' or 'ark' model of church will inevitably be less enthusiastic about 'loving our neighbour' than a 'salt and light' model.

Perhaps one of the biggest issues relates to what is often referred to as the 'prosperity gospel'. Some churches tend to stress the goodness of God in terms of the amount of prosperity he gives them, with the converse premise that if someone is not prosperous it is a sign that God does not favour them – hence giving a false justification for not caring for the poor.

WHAT ARE THE STRENGTHS AND LIMITATIONS OF CHURCH-BASED DEVELOPMENT?

We have stressed throughout these stories that the way those living in poverty can most effectively be helped is through the church. But there will inevitably be situations where this is not easy, sometimes not possible. In some areas the Christian church is not present. In some contexts the needs, the problems, are too great. Coping with earthquakes, tsunami, food shortages, war, and hurricanes can sometimes overwhelm the local church. But even then it is often the local church who are there, or the first on the scene, and can and does give vital succour and 'first aid support'.

The needs of health and education can incur big expenses, and the church through the years has a great tradition of providing these, and the associated hospitals and schools. Philippe and Donald remind us of this. However, it is often the case that small scale clinics and local schools, which need less money and are more 'human scaled', are more appropriate and can be supplied and staffed by the local church communities. It is interesting to see both Fanen and Philippe refer to the early days of their education where the schools were simple and community/church-founded. In medicine especially, there will be the need for some time for external supplies and medicines to meet on-going needs, such as ARV drugs, which cannot be met by the local church community. But often the small local clinic in each community can be more effective than the vast and expensive hospitals, often located in distant towns away from the needs of the rural communities. Kenneth has shown how, with relatively modest resources, enormous development can be made even in such 'expensive' projects as providing clean water and good hygiene, as Francis has with his national coverage of HIV/AIDs work.

We have touched in the previous section on the problem when the local church indifferent and unwelcome to the needs of the local poor. This is particularly so when the needy are 'socially unacceptable'. This used to be so for HIV/AIDS sufferers (see Joshua's stories) and still is in some churches where the members turn a blind eye to the reality of the situation. Jennifer showed that many churches were not ready to accept the women who had been prostituted. Donald has demonstrated how the Tearfund Umoja principle can be used to motivate and mobilise the local churches.

HOW CAN THE DIFFERENT 'ACTORS' IN DEVELOPMENT BEST RELATE?

Currently, there is a proliferation of actors, involved with the 'development business'. From international organisations such as the UN and WHO, to national organisations like USAID and DFID, to denominational organisations, such as CAFOD and BMS, to NGOs and CNGOs, to individual churches and organisations, and individuals with personal commitments and resources. Usually each of these works effectively in their own sphere; often they work co-operatively.

Problems can arise, however, when the underlying philosophy of the organisations differ. Should condoms be distributed in HIV/AIDs programmes? (Most secular organisations say 'yes', many churches and CNGOs say 'no'.) I was interested to see in Malawi, with Francis' work, that though they had a thorough 'behaviour change' approach to their work, they knew of, and did not discourage within marriage, the availability of condoms from the secular organisations. Joshua has also highlighted the on-going problem of the human rights debate, focussing on sexuality and preferencing the use of condoms over 'behaviour change' approaches. Should Christians pay bribes 'necessary' for actions to be facilitated? Need a CNGO compromise its plans to meet the needs of secular donor organisations like UN and DFID; should it work independently of the local church?

In practice, whereas there have been significant tensions and suspicions in the past, increasingly secular bodies, like DFID, are working alongside CNGOs, like Tearfund, as they appreciate the high quality and scope of their work. Donald spoke of the recent (2012) agreement that the UK Government made with the churches and the CNGOs, valuing and supporting the work being carried out in development by Christian organisations. It is revealing that Matthew Parris, a leading commentator in the UK, wrote an article for *The Times* entitled, 'As an atheist, I truly believe that Africa needs God', because he had seen in his travels around Malawi that the quality of Christian-lead development projects were so much better than those done by secular organisations.

HOW DO WE KNOW WE ARE MAKING A DIFFERENCE?

We discussed earlier the need for good, sensitive evaluation of development projects, lead by the communities themselves. One of the problems for CNGOs and churches is how they can professionally and sensibly evaluate their work without it being directed by the western fashion for quantitative measurement of 'impact indicators'. Many important and valid outcomes in good developments cannot be measured. This is particularly so for developments focussing on Christian transformations. Whereas it is easy to count and measure the number of wells dug in a village, it is not easy, it is not possible, to measure the spiritual, Christian changes that have occurred.

"Not every thing that can be counted, counts," as Einstein once said. Western donors want to measure everything; Africans, rightly, want to tell a story. We have included throughout this book a range of personal 'stories' which give a convincing indication of the effectiveness of their work. Yes, of course, all workers want to evaluate their work to ensure that it is as good as it can be, especially highly motivated Christian workers seeking to 'work with all their hearts, as working for the Lord, not men' (Col 3:23) – this is why so often the quality of the work of Christian NGOs and churches is better than that of secular organisation, as so many evaluations have shown.

Another problem with donor-imposed evaluation schemes is that they are inevitably time-dependent; a grant will be given for, say, two years and the evaluation must be made at the end of that time. In practice, of course, real development is an on-going process with no nice tidy end, and real development within communities is unpredictable. As Donald discusses with the Umoja process, there is considerable time spend mobilising the church and the community before it is clear what they want to be working on together, and this early stage is invaluable and essential. To support such work, resources need to be given in trust, without clear preconceptions – not something which donors, with their demands for financial accountability, find easy. Conversely, the temporary nature of many non-church interventions can be disillusioning for the participants. I was saddened by Irene's quote of the women in her Zambian compound complaining that previous researchers had had no commitment to them but "just came, asked them questions and went away." Local churches do not 'go away'.

Furthermore, and this is central to a Christian's motivation, we are called not to be successful but to do our best and to do what is right. Irene spoke of the microfinance worker who chose to work not with the poorest of the poor but the entrepreneurial poor who were more likely to give her successful results. Jesus sought to serve and to love those in need, not those who might provide measurable impact indicators. So our question remains how can we evaluate our work in a way which is valid according to our objectives? How can we satisfy, or change, those donor organisations who insist on measurable outcomes for everything? Fortunately, church-based work utilising the local communities' resources, which does not rely on external donor funding, is spared this.

WHAT CAN WELL-MEANING OUTSIDERS DO?

The more I see of the work that local churches can do to develop their own communities, and the more I see western outsiders going out to give aid to 'the poor in Africa', to 'sort out their problems', the more uncertain I am that all the western help is actually helpful. It is so easy to cause dependency and introduce different, foreign, destructive values. A Christian leader of an AIC church recently said to a largely western audience in London, when asked what the west could do to help, said, "Just give us a level playing field, and then leave us to get on with it." A Sudanese Bishop said on receiving a grant to build a clinic, "You give us a shove to get us started and we will carry on from there."

The disturbing book *When Helping Hurts*, from two leading evangelical Americans, sums up in its title the potential dangers of well-meaning, compassionate Christians working out their own personal agendas, not always to the benefit of the recipients.

Let me try and address this question as I have had to for myself, and leave it to others to tackle for themselves, for their organisations, in their context.

- Simple but true: the first thing that can be done is to pray for the needy communities around the world. We are engaged in spiritual battles (Eph 6:12). Organising and co-ordinating prayer support across the world is a vital further contribution.
- Secondly, to get informed about the situation, to listen to the locals, to hear *their* cry. For the professionals this will mean making scoping exercises, for the individual it will often mean personal visits, usually organised by one of the trusted CNGOs. The prime purpose then is not to give but to gain, to observe, and to learn what inspirational and resourceful Christians there are. Personal experience can change one's perspective like none other. Human resources are not in short supply in Africa. Sometimes local factors restrict such resources being fully utilised.
- Providing money, resources, and expertise from the affluent west to the poorer regions of the world is clearly appropriate in some situations. But, before providing money too readily, we must consider the possibility of distorting the local economy, of causing dependency, of corrupting local values, and of doing more harm

than good. Such harm has been seen both at the individual and the governmental level. Western money *can* go so much further in, say, Africa than in the west. When I first realised that £20, the price of a good meal in the west, was sufficient to pay the salary of a teacher or a nurse in Zambia for one month (when in the UK that would cost £2,000, 100 times more), my perspective on money changed. In some cases, specialist expertise is invaluable, both to stimulate, and supplement local resources. But again the donor needs to beware of being the person who 'knows best', and in so doing makes the recipient take on a 'victim' role, become dependent and undermines local resourcefulness and self-confidence.

- And fourthly, we can advocate, we can fight for justice. "Speak up for those who cannot speak for themselves, for the rights of all who are destitute" (Prov 31.8). So much of the fundamental causes of poverty and gross inequality around the world are due to bad governance and unjust legislation at both the national and the international level. The church through her organisational structures, through the para-church of CNGOs, and through her individual members can and does advocate against injustice at national and international levels. In the UK we have had the Jubilee 2000 and the Make Poverty History campaigns and they have had considerable success, especially in the cancellation of the crippling national debts for many of the poorest countries. We are now, 2013, starting the national *IF* campaign: "There is enough food in the world for every one, IF…."

END PIECE

As I have been finishing this piece, the new Pope Francis has been inaugurated in Rome. He stressed the need for the church to have compassion, and to care, for the poor, but he added that the church's role must be more than this, or 'it would be reduced to the role of a well-meaning NGO'. The church must preach and demonstrate the whole gospel, the holistic gospel, healing the soul as well as the body. A fitting message for this book, which emphasises the message that full community transformation can only come through the work of the local church, with whom the CNGOs can work together.

Conclusions and Outstanding Issues

In this small book we have sought to bring together, and celebrate, examples from practitioner development experts working in Africa. We have been aware that we have raised, hopefully clarified, many still unresolved issues. But we hope that we have given some indications of the best way forward, through 'listening to the poor' and working with and through the local churches who are motivated to share the holistic gospel with the poor and needy. We hope that these good news stories from Africa, illustrating community development through the churches, will indeed bring glory to God and relief and shalom to many in our suffering world.

SELECTED BIBLIOGRAPHY

Alkire, S and Newell, E (eds), *What Can One Person Do? Faith to Heal a Broken World* (London: Darton, Longman and Todd Ltd, 2005).

Alkire, S and Deneuline, S, 'The human development and capability approach, in Deneuline, S and Shahani, L (eds), *An Introduction to Human Development and Capability Approach; Freedom and Agency* (Earthscan, 2009)

Chester, T, *Good News to the Poor: Sharing the Gospel through Social Involvement* (Leicester: IVP, 2004).

Chuhan-Pole, P, and Angwafo, M (eds), *Yes, Africa Can: Success Stories from a Dynamic Continent* (Washington: The World Bank, 2011).

Corbett, S and Fikkert, B, *When Helping Hurts* (Chicago: Moody Publishers, 2009).

Ditcher T and Harper M (eds), *What is Wrong with Microfinance?* (Intermediate Technology Publications Ltd, 2007).

Grant, P, *Poor No More* (Oxford:, Monach Books, 2008).

Hopper, P, *Understanding Development* (Cambridge: Polity Press, 2012).

Keshomshahara, A, *A Theology of Poverty Reduction in Tanzania* (Dodoma: Central Tanganyika Press, 2008).

Merideth M, *The State of Africa: A History of the Continent Since Independence* (London: Simon and Schuster, 2011).

Monser, J, *Gender and Development* (Abingdon: Routledge, 2010).

Moyo, D, *Dead Aid* (London: Penguin, 2009).

Narayan D, Chambers R, Shah MK, and Petesch P, *Voices of the Poor Crying Out for Change* (World Bank. Oxford: Oxford University Press, 2011).

Parris, M, 'As an atheist, I truly believe Africa needs God', *The Times* 2008.

Roche, C, *Impact Assessment for Development Agencies: Learning to Value Change* (Oxford: Oxfam, 1999).

Sen, A, *Development as Freedom* (Oxford: Oxford University Press, 2001).

Woolnough, B, 'But how do we know we are making a difference?' *Transformation* 25.2 & 3 (2008), 134-143.

Woolnough, B and Ma, W (eds), *Holistic Mission: God's plan for God's People* (Oxford: Regnu, 2010).

RECENT REGNUM TITLES

Regnum Edinburgh Centenary Series

A Learning Missional Church: Reflections from Young Missiologists
Beate Fagerli, Knud Jørgensen, Rolv Olsen, Kari Storstein Haug and Knut Tveitereid (Eds)
2012 / 978-1-908355-01-1 / 218pp (hardback)
Cross-cultural mission has always been a primary learning experience for the church. It pulls us out of a mono-cultural understanding and helps us discover a legitimate theological pluralism which opens up for new perspectives in the Gospel. Translating the Gospel into new languages and cultures is a human and divine means of making us learn new 'incarnations' of the Good News.

Mission Spirituality and Authentic Discipleship
Wonsuk Ma and Kenneth R Ross (Eds)
2013 / 978-1-908355-24-9 / 274pp (hardback)
This book argues for the primacy of spirituality in the practice of mission. Since God is the primary agent of mission and God works through the power of the Holy Spirit, it is through openness to the Spirit that mission finds its true character and has its authentic impact. This is demonstrated today particularly by movements of Christian faith in the global south which carry the good news to the heart of communities in every part of the world. Originating in the Edinburgh 2010 mission study project, the essays assembled in this volume show that today there is a renewal of the missionary impetus of the churches which is marked by its spiritual character. Here fresh motivation for mission is being found, moving people of faith to share the good news of Jesus Christ both within their own communities and by crossing frontiers to take the message to new contexts.

Regnum Studies In Global Christianity

Contemporary Pentecostal Christianity: Interpretations from an African Context
J Kwabena Asamoah-Gyada
2013 / 978-1-908355-07-2 / 238pp

Pentecostalism is the fastest growing stream of Christianity in the world. The real evidence for the significance of Pentecostalism lies in the actual churches they have built and the numbers they attract. This work interprets key theological and missiological themes in African Pentecostalism by using material from the live experiences of the movement itself.

From this World to the Next: Christian Identity and Funerary Rites in Nepal
Bal Krishna Sharma
2013 / 978-1-908355-08-9 / 238pp
This book explores and analyses funerary rite struggles in a nation where Christianity is a comparatively recent phenomenon, and many families have multi-faith, who go through traumatic experiences at the death of their family members. The author has used an applied theological approach to explore and analyse the findings in order to address the issue of funerary rites with which the Nepalese church is struggling.

Regnum Studies In Mission

Searching for Heaven in the Real World: A Sociological Discussion of Conversion in the Arab World
Kathryn Kraft
2012 / 978-1-908355-15-7 / 1428pp
Kathryn Kraft explores the breadth of psychological and social issues faced by Arab Muslims after making a decision to adopt a faith in Christ or Christianity, investigating some of the most surprising and significant challenges new believers face.

Proclaiming the Peacemaker: The Malaysian Church as an Agent of Reconciliation in a Multicultural Society
Peter Rowan
2012 / 978-1-908355-05-8 / 268pp
With a history of racial violence and in recent years, low-level ethnic tensions, the themes of peaceful coexistence and social harmony are recurring ones in the discourse of Malaysian society. In such a context, this book looks at the role of the church as a reconciling agent, arguing that a reconciling presence within a divided society necessitates an ethos of peacemaking.

Regnum Books International

Regnum is an Imprint of The Oxford Centre for Mission Studies
St. Philip and St. James Church, Woodstock Road, Oxford, OX2 6HR
For full listing go to: www.ocms.ac.uk/regnum